"Fran is spot-on with her delightfu
manager! *Fair Lady* also brough†
knowing Fran through the IAFE wh.
was well-respected for her drive and passion for the Monroe Couy
Fair. This book will resonate with "fair folk" and provide insight to our
friends, family, and neighbors about the crazy life we lead!"

–Marla J. Calico, President & CEO, International Association
of Fairs & Expositions (and former manager of the
Ozark Empire Fair, Springfield, Missouri)

"This well-written book is a delight and will amuse county fair folk
everywhere with Fran's memories of her time spent as executive
director of the Monroe County Fair. All fairs have had to deal in one
way or another with the type of problems described here, but few
people have faced their "challenges" with the spunk and feistiness
that Fran has described. I was employed by the New York State
Department of Agriculture and Markets for many years, where part
of my job was to serve as a liaison with New York's county and youth
fairs. It was always a pleasure to deal with Fran and to watch her work
so hard to gradually make the Monroe County Fair an entity that was
well-respected by local, state, and national fair and entertainment
industries."

–Gail Fuller, Associate Budget Analyst, NYS Department of
Agriculture & Markets, Division of Fiscal Management

"A great read. Fran was a pioneer and role model for female fair
executives in an industry dominated by males in the 90s. Her thirst
for operations knowledge and marketing/promotion ideas was never-
ending."

–Robert W. Johnson, Retired President & CEO,
Outdoor Amusement Business Association

"*Fair Lady* is a humorous collection of the good, bad, and yes, the sometimes ugly! Those of us who have Fair Fever, myself for over forty years, will delight and chuckle as the stories unfold, many of which have been experienced first-hand. The Fair Lady herself is a pioneer in the business for her achievements and leadership professionalism in a time of change. *Fair Lady* is an awesome personal account and a wonderful 'snap shot' of the importance of the county fair! What a great ride! Bravo, Fran, it's all 'Lollipops and Roses!'"

–Russell Marquart, CFE, Executive Secretary,
NYS Association of Agricultural Fairs, Inc.

"While so many of us enjoy the fun and excitement of fairs, few know of the hard work, anxiety-inducing situations, and often plain luck that go into producing these iconic community celebrations. *Fair Lady* provides a unique glimpse into the massive planning, the creative and sometimes on-the-fly solutions, plus the serendipity that provide a winning recipe for those brave enough to take on management of a fair. *Fair Lady* is a laugh-out-loud read highlighting some of the unique and sometimes crazy situations that fair managers face."

–Margaret O'Neill, former Monroe County 4-H Program Leader

"What a great book! I enjoyed reading and reflecting on the challenges and rewarding experiences in the fair business. The mixture of humor and hardship is a good reminder to focus on the goals rather than trying to please others. The hard work and dedication pays off with witnessing the smiles and shared love of the fair. Thanks to Fran for recording her memories of what it takes to have a successful fair."

–Edward T Rossley, 1st Vice President,
NYS Association of Agricultural Fairs, Inc.

"*Fair Lady* accurately describes the roller coaster ride of fair management: the highs, the lows, the twists and turns, and even the upside-down moments. Fran's raw emotions, thoughts, and feelings, coupled with her sense of humor, leave the reader with compassion for her struggles and successes while giggling at the same time. Her efforts to make the Monroe County Fair great shine through—even through the 'damn roof!'"

–Jessica Underberg, CFE, Erie County Fair, CEO,
Past President, NYS Association of Agricultural Fairs, Inc.
Past International Association of Fairs and Expos Chair

Fair Lady

Memoirs of a County Fair Manager

Fair Lady

MEMOIRS OF A
COUNTY FAIR MANAGER

Frances I. Tepper, CFE

COSMOGRAPHIA BOOKS
ROCHESTER, NY

Copyright © 2021 by Frances Tepper. All rights reserved.
Published by Cosmographia Books, Rochester, NY

No part of this publication may be reproduced, distributed, or transmitted in any form or by any means, including photocopying, recording, or other electronic or mechanical methods, without the prior written permission of the publisher, except in the case of brief quotations embodied in critical reviews and certain other noncommercial uses permitted by copyright law.

This book is a memoir. It reflects the author's present recollection of experiences over time. Some names and characteristics have been changed or modified, some events have been compressed, and some dialogue has been recreated.

Cover and interior design by Nina Alvarez
Cover art by Eunice Stahl
Frontispiece photo by Bill Pfeifer
Author photo by Red Purse Marketing

For permission to reprint portions of this book, or to order a review copy, contact editor@cosmographiabooks.com

ISBN: 978-0-578-91692-7

Contents

Fair Lady is dedicated to all the fair staff who, over the years, devised
ways to do the impossible and found solutions for the unsolvable.
You are all rock stars!

Prologue

It was early—too early to be at the fairgrounds. I had left only a few hours before, the moon already high in its arc across the sky, when I finally closed the door to my hotel room. The hotel was close to the fairgrounds, and I liked being there. It was easier than driving home late at night after the fair closed. I could unwind without thoughts of dirty dishes or unmade beds. When I closed the door, the cacophony of the county fair faded away. I always gave a sigh as the door clicked shut, the quiet embracing me like a warm blanket.

But tonight, I couldn't sleep. After months of planning layouts, food choices, and entertainment, after hosting 30,000 people, some of whom were delightful and others not so much, after a week of unrelenting challenges, smiles, tears, complaints, wins, and losses, the county fair was over. My head was filled with images that ran like a movie reel in my head. This had been my last fair as manager. It was time to retire, time to step back from the history and the pageantry of the fair world and to let a new generation put its mark on the annual event.

I stood outside in front of my office. The air was crisp this early in the day, the cool breath of autumn already hovering. Although it was quiet now, I could hear the echo of music from the carousel and the distinctive whooshing of the Giant Claw as it swung, spinning its shrieking occupants, defying death with every terrifying revolution. The ripe aroma of the cattle barn permeated the morning air, and flies buzzed noisily, calling their colleagues to join in the feasting of the rich manure.

For a fair manager, there is nothing sadder than the morning after the fair. The food vendors have all pulled in their awnings and hitched up their trailers, already moving on, anticipating their next destinations. The carnival workers, like magicians, have dismantled the rides in only a few hours, so that by morning, all that remains is fair detritus: stray red cups that roll down the depleted midway like tumbleweed, upended popcorn boxes whose contents are greedily consumed by a flock of seagulls, and a lone balloon, still tied to a pole, a gay bit of color in the now barren landscape. I often wondered from where the seagulls came. We were nowhere near the sea. Perhaps they are gypsy birds that follow the carnivals from place to place, knowing there will be good eating in their wake.

Only a week ago, we scurried, preparing the fairgrounds for our guests. There were flowers to plant, a horse arena to till, livestock pens to assemble, tables to set up, permits and licenses to secure, inspections to endure, and tents and flags, signs and decorations to place as we put our best foot forward. We had such high hopes—for no rain, for no scorching heat, for record crowds, for a community event that would be both fun and profitable for everyone. And now, it was time to undo everything: to scrub the livestock barns, to dispose of manure, to sweep, and grade, and dismantle, to reconcile the books, and finally, to evaluate. It was over, the good and the bad. And yet, as I looked out over the grounds that morning, I knew my heart wasn't ready to let it all go. I had twenty years of memories crowding my mind: some happy, some sad, some funny, and some funny only in retrospect.

CHAPTER ONE

Life's Twisty Roller Coaster

My parents were Sicilian immigrants. Both were children when their families left Sicily in search of better economic opportunities than could be found in their small, rural towns. They traveled through Ellis Island and finally settled in Rochester, New York. Since they came from a temperate, Mediterranean climate, I often wondered why they chose to live in a place where winters lasted seven months and spring was only wishful thinking, but settle in Rochester they did, and there they stayed.

Rochester is the third largest city in New York State. Located on the southern shore of Lake Ontario, it is more conservative and Midwestern than East Coast. Even the way we pronounce our words make us sound more like Chicagoans than New Yorkers. For many years, being the headquarters of the "Big Three" (Eastman Kodak, Xerox, and Bausch and Lomb) defined the area, attracting a highly educated population that had a strong technological bent. But it was also home to large immigrant populations that changed over time from Italian and Irish to Eastern European to Southeast Asian to Puerto Rican.

The Italian families that came to Rochester in the early twentieth century congregated in enclaves, maintaining their traditions and their native tongue. Being suspicious of "outsiders," they typically married others from their homeland. My parents were no exception. My mother wed when she was nineteen and my father twenty-three, their union producing four children: three daughters and a son who died at age five, before I was born.

I was the youngest child in a very traditional Italian family. When I was growing up, we never went to our county fair, even though it had been around since 1823. It wasn't even in our frame of reference. Our lives revolved around the church, which was next door, our grandmother's house, which was down the street, and school, which was also down the street. On those rare times when we ventured out of the neighborhood, it was to take a Sunday drive with my family (during which my father invariably got lost), or to take a bus to Charlotte Beach with my Aunt Mary, or to walk a mile with my cousins to the Webster Theater to see an Esther Williams film. On a few wondrous occasions, my father would announce that we were going to Seabreeze, a local amusement park. My heart would pound with excitement as we arrived, and I'd jump up and down with pent-up energy until I got on my first ride. I particularly loved the historic carousel that was brought to the park in 1926. I would ride the hand-carved, majestic horses over and over until I was dizzy, longing for the day when I would be big enough to reach the brass ring.

Every Saturday, my family and I would go to the local public market to buy our produce for the week's meals. I loved the sights, sounds, and smells of the market: the pungent aroma of the cheeses and sausages, the squawking of the chickens that would be in someone's stew pot by dinnertime, and the bushels of vibrantly colored fruits and vegetables that my father would scrutinize, gently squeezing, smelling, and sometimes even tasting the fruits to determine if they were ripe enough or sweet enough for our table.

Once a year, my family would go on an expedition to Roy and Frieda's farm. Frieda's chickens supplied eggs for my uncle's grocery store, and Roy grew vegetables for the produce department. It took anywhere from one-and-a-half to three hours to get to the farm, depending on how lost my father was. (He had no sense of direction but always insisted he knew the way.) All I remember about those excursions was that the chickens smelled and that Roy gave my sister and me a ride on his tractor, causing my mother to pace until we were safely deposited back on the firmament. The farmers market and the farm excursions were my only contacts with agriculture. Basically,

I was a city girl, surrounded only by family and familiar city sights.

My sheltered life in the city changed quite abruptly at age nine when my mother died of rheumatic heart disease. She was only forty-six, and a "simple" heart valve replacement would have afforded her a normal lifespan. But in 1954, the procedure was still experimental and not an option for her. My father, a pack-a-day Camel smoker who never really recovered from my mother's death, succumbed to lung cancer seven years later when I was a senior in high school. My sisters had already left home and were living in California, so the period following his death was a lonely and tumultuous time for me. I lived with an aunt and uncle for several months until the end of the school year. Then I packed whatever of my belongings I could fit into two suitcases and boarded a train to California, bidding a very tearful farewell to my high school sweetheart. (I cried for the entire 3,000 mile trip, much to the consternation of the people sitting around me.) In California, I began a new life in a much bigger and vastly different world from the one I had known.

Still, I had a plan I was intent on following. I was determined to go to college, despite the fact that I had absolutely no money for tuition or housing. I applied to the University of Southern California (USC) and was thrilled to be accepted there. I was even more thrilled when they offered me a scholarship, making it possible for me to actually attend. I had always planned on majoring in journalism, and USC had a good journalism school, so I felt that I was finally on my way to the life I had planned. I had visions of becoming a foreign correspondent and venturing into war zones for cutting-edge reporting—until the head of the journalism department told me that the only job for women in journalism was writing for the society page. This was in the early 1960s. So, since I really liked and did well in geology, I decided to go into that field instead—until the head of the geology department told me that there was no future in geology for women unless I wanted to teach. Ultimately, I majored in sociology. That, apparently, was an "acceptable" field for women. I finally had a pathway to the future even though it was a much different pathway than the one I had anticipated.

I didn't forget or lose touch with my high school sweetheart (the one I had cried over for 3,000 miles), and we were married right after I graduated from college. I headed back to Rochester, and we started married life in a ten-by-fifty-five foot trailer that we stubbornly insisted on calling a mobile home. We also acquired a stray black cat who had enormous paws and who liked to hide under our bed and attack me whenever I walked past. Almost immediately, I started sneezing and coughing. An allergist told me that I was not only allergic to the cat, but also to cows, sheep, goats, rabbits, horses, chickens, dogs, and alfalfa and timothy hay. We found a new home for the cat, and I figured I didn't have to worry about the rest. After all, I lived in the city, and I was a social worker. Not a cow in sight.

But that would change. Two kids later, my husband was transferred to Santa Maria, a small town on the central California coast. At that time, the town was so tiny that there was only one building tall enough to have an escalator. The foot of the escalator became the town's meeting place because everybody knew exactly where it was.

There were four things that almost everyone in Santa Maria supported: summer theater, rodeo (preceded by a parade that lasted three hours), the Santa Claus Parade (that lasted three minutes), and the Santa Barbara County Fair. We had only been in town for a few days when the fair opened, so like good Santa Marians, we packed up our two little girls and went to the fair.

Santa Maria and the surrounding area is strawberry country where berries are harvested from April to December—quite a change from the two-week strawberry-growing season to which we New Yorkers were accustomed. We found that strawberries in their various forms were plentiful throughout the fair, from jams and jellies to baked goods. In the 4-H building, the 4-H kids handed out samples of huge, juicy berries they had grown. Our appetites whetted, we stopped at the Mormon Church booth where they served homemade strawberry pie. The crust was flaky, the whipped cream real, and the berries the sweetest on earth. I've never been able to duplicate that pie.

Next we sampled corn, salty and dripping with butter, that had been picked just hours before. In retrospect, we pretty much ate our way through the fair, testing out the fried dough and seeing if "the best Italian sausage" really was.

Deciding we needed to walk off some calories, we wandered into the Commercial Building. The only person we knew in Santa Maria was the Culligan Man, who had hooked up our water softener. When we spotted him at his booth, he greeted us as if we were his best friends. Suddenly, we felt like we belonged in our new town. We knew somebody! Because we were naive, we signed up for drawings for a set of encyclopedias, for waterless cookware, for an amazing knife set that never needed sharpening, and for an all-expense-paid Caribbean cruise. Soon we knew a lot more people in town, all of whom wanted to sell us something.

Then it was off to the livestock barn, the first time my very urban kids had seen farm animals. They watched as a cow was milked, amazed that milk didn't originate in the grocery store, and they wondered aloud if brown cows gave chocolate milk. When we came to the beef cattle area, I explained that those animals provided us with steak and hamburgers. As the kids seemed perplexed by this, I decided not to elaborate on how that actually occurred. A farmer shearing sheep came next, and they gaped at the process and asked if it hurt the sheep to get a haircut. Holding their noses in the pig barn, they giggled at a greedy sow that had her head stuck in her feed bucket and then *oohed* and *ahhed* over the nursing piglets. Our last stop was at the rabbit barn, where the bunnies were just the right size for petting. It was the highlight of the livestock area for the kids, and we had to bribe them with ice cream to get them to leave.

We concluded our trip to the fair at the carnival where the kiddie rides thrilled my girls. My oldest daughter rode the "little horsies" many times, beginning her life-long love for that animal. For months afterward, I could always tell where she was by listening for the sounds of her "neighs" as she galloped around the playground. As she grew older and got into riding real horses, which was a very expensive and somewhat dangerous hobby, I often wished she had focused instead on some other aspect of the fair—like pie-making.

We went to the fair every year of the four years we lived in Santa Maria. The horses and the bunnies were our favorite animals, and we always headed straight for those barns (after the strawberry pie booth.) Going to that fair was the highlight of our summers. It was something we could do as a family that was wholesome, fun and, well, delicious. But eventually my husband was transferred back to Rochester, so kicking and screaming the whole way, we left the fair behind us.

Three years later, my son was born, much to the dismay of my (now) middle child who was convinced that he would usurp her place in my affections. To bribe her into accepting her new baby brother, my husband and I decided to get her a rabbit, something she had been bugging us about since she had first seen them at the fair in Santa Maria. Having been exposed to 4-H at that fair, we thought the 4-H Youth Development Program would be a good place for her to learn about the animal, so we enrolled her in a 4-H rabbit club. With her orange Netherland Dwarf tucked firmly under her chin, she went to her first club meeting. Since I was the driver, I tagged along.

The family room of the 4-H leader's house was overflowing with twenty kids, both boys and girls, ranging in age from seven to seventeen. Each kid held one or more rabbits. Some had Netherland Dwarfs like my daughter, some held lop-eared bunnies, and one girl had several fluffy white Angoras. We learned that the kids were into breeding their rabbits, something we had never even considered, but as we investigated, we were soon intrigued by the idea and by the color varieties found in each new litter.

"Let's breed Caramel once to see what color babies we get," I said to my husband. And the die was cast. We fell in love with the little bunnies. That is how we eventually ended up with two hundred rabbits in our basement and, for the next ten years, a small business called The Rabbitat that the kids ran. Besides learning responsibility, animal husbandry, and entrepreneurship, I never had to give my kids "the sex talk." Watching the rabbits breed took care of that.

I eventually took over as leader of the Curious Critters 4-H Rabbit and Cavy (guinea pig) Club that now boasted forty-plus members, and I became known as "The Rabbit Lady." Not only did I have fun with the kids (all of my kids were now in 4-H), but I also learned about rabbits right along with them.

Our rabbit project took us to the Monroe County Fair. We began showing our bunnies and working in the barn, helping with the shows. But even though Rochester was far larger than Santa Maria, both in population and in square miles, the Monroe County Fair was a disappointment. There was little agriculture, it was expensive, and it had a reputation for fights.

My association with the rabbit club and my volunteer duties at the fair eventually led me to a job with Cornell Cooperative Extension where I worked as a 4-H program assistant. At that time, 4-H had had a falling out with the fair board and was holding its own youth fair in an alternate location, a solution that was detrimental to both the fair and to 4-H. I asked to become a liaison to the fair board with the hope of mending fences and getting 4-H back to its traditional place at the fair.

It was the late 1980s, and, as I recall, the fair board was comprised of twenty-three members: seventeen men and six women, including me. The board president was the chief of police at one of the nearby towns. Most of the men on the board were well into their sixties and had been members for a good many years. In contrast, most of the women were fairly new and were in their late thirties or early forties. At best, the male board members tolerated the newcomers, but they bristled at the inevitable challenges to their traditions. One of the women was an attorney, and she was constantly questioning decisions and reports. I remember one meeting in particular that got quite contentious. Finally, the president sat back in his chair and casually opened his jacket so we could see his service revolver. That intimidated all of us except for the attorney, who was unlikely to ever back away from a fight. Since we were in an unheated upstairs room in the middle of winter, I left that meeting shivering from the cold, the tension, and the intimidation.

Four years later, I had gotten 4-H back to the fair and had worked my way into the job of chair of the fair committee as well as vice president of the board. Simultaneously, the president of the board and the executive director became ill with terminal cancer. Both resigned. That left me in charge with only four months to go until fair. I took a leave of absence from Cooperative Extension and became immersed in planning the upcoming fair as well as directing the activities at the Fair Association's event center, both of which were totally new experiences for me. After a successful fair in 1992, the board offered me a permanent position.

And that's how, after many twists and turns, a would-be foreign correspondent who was allergic to livestock became the first female executive director of the 169-year-old, good ole boys' network known as the Monroe County Fair and Recreation Association. It was a job I never envisioned, but it was the one that would come to define me.

CHAPTER TWO

The Lot

Location! Location! Location! It's everything if you're running a brick and mortar business. Unfortunately, the location of the Monroe County Fair sucked. It was midway between two of the biggest fairs in the country: the Erie County Fair in Hamburg (near Buffalo) and the New York State Fair in Syracuse. If local people thought about the fair, which they rarely did, it was one of those two, not the one in their own county.

The fairgrounds (called "the lot" in carnival jargon) were on a sixty-acre tract of land in Henrietta, a suburb of Rochester. When the fairgrounds were purchased in 1947, the land was in the middle of nowhere. When I was a kid, I remember my family taking Sunday drives to Henrietta because the Meisenzahl Dairy, which was located in the town, had the best black raspberry ice cream in the county. It took us a long time to get to Meisenzahl's, probably because my father had no clue how to get there. At that time, there were few residences or businesses in the area, and the land was mostly used for farming.

As the years passed, Henrietta grew into a densely populated and highly commercialized town, including the area directly across the street from the fairgrounds. Instead of having cornfields for neighbors, the fairgrounds were now in the center of a residential area. The neighbors did not particularly like living in close proximity to the fairgrounds and continually complained about the noise (smell, traffic, etc.) This drove me crazy because we had first dibs. After all, the fairgrounds were there long before any of the houses were built.

The town supervisor, who hated having the fairgrounds in his town, called it "an eyesore." I took issue with that, although I will admit that it wasn't particularly pretty and did not look like a park. I prefer to say it was "rustic," as are most fairgrounds.

There were five buildings in all: three old, metal buildings in the front of the fairgrounds, mostly used for storage, and two buildings about a quarter of a mile from the county road. The main building was a 25,000 square foot domed arena, the prototype for many of the domed arenas that would spring up around the country (most of which have wisely been demolished.) It was an unfortunate design for the Northeast. In the winter, the snow avalanched off the sloped roof and tore the membrane that covered the wooden structure beneath it. As a result, the roof leaked almost from day one and nothing ever repaired it permanently.

Dome in 2021

The Dome was a two-story structure. The arena was on the main floor, and upstairs there was a large (unheated) conference room and two small meeting rooms. But the most interesting upstairs room was the chapel. The room was conceptualized and sponsored by the Projansky family. The Projansky patriarch was a prominent Rochester furrier and a one-time member of the fair's board of directors. I was told that the chapel came about because Mr. Projanski wanted the Dome to have a place that would be available to anyone who wanted to get married, regardless of religious affiliation. The prevailing belief was that the chapel was designed as a round room so "the devil couldn't corner you." It was darkly paneled, and since it was an interior space, there were no windows. It was really rather creepy. My longest-tenured secretary refused to go into it.

Connected to the Dome by a dark and narrow passage was Minett Hall, a 21,000 square foot rectangular metal-and-cinderblock building. Both edifices had originally been built to be ice arenas, but the energy crunch hit just when they were completed, and it became financially impossible to run them as intended. The ice was never used in the Dome and was used for only a few years in Minett Hall, much to the disgust of the neighbors who never forgave the Fair Association for "taking away their ice." (More about that later.) The buildings were repurposed as event centers and were rented out for shows and conventions. They also became the primary buildings for the fair.

Along the county road that ran in front of the fairgrounds, was an oval, short (under a mile) motorsport track. In the 1950s, it was one of the premier stock car tracks in the country, hosting major national NASCAR races, with race winners including Lee Petty (father of Richard Petty), Tim Flock, and Cotton Owens—the who's who of early racing greats. But because of the residential buildup, the noise and dust from the track became problematic. In 1958, NASCAR hosted its last race, although weekly stock car races did run until 1961. Thereafter, the track was used only at fair time.[1]

When the track was built, wooden grandstand bleachers were installed that seated about 7,000 people. It is my understanding that the bleachers were not new when they were brought to the fairgrounds. By the time I became executive director, some of the tiers had been demolished, and those that were left were now at least fifty years old and built long before any of the current safety regulations were in place. They stood about twenty feet high, there were no backs to the seats, and there were large gaps between the rows of seats. A small child could easily fall through the openings. I constantly worried about this safety hazard, but our insurance carrier didn't seem to have an issue with it.

Sometime in the late 1990s, we changed insurance companies,

and a risk manager came to inspect the grandstand. It was about two weeks before the fair when our insurance agent notified us that the company would not ensure the grandstand unless we made some significant improvements to it. What they wanted amounted to a complete rebuild of the bleachers to eliminate any gaps. This would not only be cost prohibitive, but there was also no way it could be accomplished before the fair.

After considering many options, none of which we had the time or money to do, I hit on the idea of using snow fencing. We could staple the fencing to the bottom of each tier of the bleachers and effectively create a safety net. We could also attach it to the sides and backs to prevent people from falling. I presented this idea to the insurance company, and they agreed to allow it. That was the first hurdle. The second hurdle was finding enough snow fencing in the middle of summer to accomplish the task. This was long before Amazon shopping, so we had to travel far and wide as we searched for stores that still had some fencing left after the winter. The third hurdle was getting enough volunteers to do the job. Surprisingly, that was the easiest of them all since I was able to get inmates from a nearby state prison to augment help from our fair volunteers. It turned out to be a fairly easy fix that took only about a half-day and several cases of beer to complete. The orange fencing didn't look pretty, but it did solve the problem.

In front of the grandstand was a sixteen-foot high safety fence that was designed to prevent debris and tires from flying into the grandstand during track events. After many years, the fence had rusted and looked terrible, so we decided to paint it silver, the color of most new fences. It looked great—all silvery and shiny. Unfortunately the grandstand faced northwest, so when the sun started to set, it shined directly on the fencing. The silver color reflected the sun, completely blinding the people in the grandstand and making it impossible for them to see anything that was happening on the track. Dealing with the complaints of an unhappy demolition derby crowd (mob) was not something I wanted to repeat, so the next year, we repainted the fence, this time using black paint, which was counterintuitive. However, it worked and no one complained, at least not about the fence.

Behind the track was an outdoor horse arena, although the footing was not up to professional standards, and the riders never failed to complain to me about it. The rest of the sixty acres was used for parking.

A creek ran through the fairgrounds, and on the other side of the creek was a beautiful, wildflower meadow that was surrounded by scrub trees and shrubs, along with deer, a multitude of rabbits, and even a fox or two. Of course, since it was pretty secluded, it was also a lovers' lane, a high school hangout, and a dumping ground, especially for used tires. Once, we found a burned-out washing machine. When we renovated the fairgrounds in 2006, we also found and plowed under a thriving patch of marijuana plants, but no one ever admitted ownership of that particular agricultural endeavor.

While I was executive director of the fairgrounds, we sold the front parcel of land to a local grocery store chain. This eliminated the three ugly metal buildings as well as the track. A new, smaller track was built in the meadow. Sheltered by scrub trees that provided a sound barrier from the noise of the events, it was the perfect location, even if we did displace the rabbits.

When we moved the track, we actually sold the old grandstand, which was now at least sixty-five years old, to another fair. I think the cost of refurbishing it was probably more expensive than buying or renting new metal bleachers that were up to regulation, but the other fair's officials insisted they had the people-power to do the job. We were glad to get rid of the bleachers, especially since the volunteers from the other fair took care of dismantling them. The paint on them was beyond peeling, the metal support structure was rusted, and the wooden planks were warped, so I was very glad I was not a member of the crew charged with fixing them.

Ready! Set! Go!

Some things I learned at my first fair:

- You need a permit from the town if you're going to blow up something during a grandstand event. If you don't, the fire marshal will show up at your door with official-looking papers that say things about fines and jail time.

- Don't put the Right to Life booth next to the Planned Parenthood booth.

- People will go where they want to go. Trying to change the traffic pattern is useless.

- Vendors come back to fairs year after year and expect to be in the same locations. Messing with that is taking your life in your hands.

- As fair manager, if it rains and people don't come, it's your fault. It's also your fault if it's too hot or too cold or if, on opening day of the fair, the local newspaper decides to do a front page story on carnival ride accidents.

- If you want to eat supper at the Grange booth, order your food at lunchtime. It should be ready by dinnertime.

- Anything that can go wrong usually happens in the last fifteen minutes of the day, just when you thought you were home free.

Somehow, we managed to put the fair together in four months. Since I was hired as executive director on a temporary basis, I was determined that this fair would be a great one so the board would have no choice but to offer me a permanent position. Because I didn't have any notion of how things had always been done, I proceeded to design the layout the way I thought it should be, moving events and vendors around willy-nilly. This was not a wise choice. Some displaced vendors actually threatened that this would be my first and last fair . . . if I actually made it to the end of the week.

Not only was I new to the fair, but we also had a new carnival. The company was young but in the process of growing into what would become Powers Great American Midways, one of the premier carnivals in the country. But then it was still Amusements of Rochester, and Corky, the owner, was very eager to play his hometown fair. I went to visit Corky at some of his other locations, and I was impressed. The rides seemed to sparkle. They were meticulously maintained, and the company's safety record was excellent, a very important point to somebody who worried excessively about everything. My biggest fear was that we would have a serious ride accident.

The fairgrounds were very large and sprawling with no clear traffic pattern except for tradition. I wanted to use one of the metal buildings in the front of the fairgrounds to house the commercial and nonprofit exhibits, so I ignored warnings that people would not go to that building because it was too far from the midway. I proceeded to put the exhibitors in what I thought was a perfectly fine building in a perfectly fine area.

As predicted, few people found their way to that building, giving the idle vendors ample time to work up their animosity, especially Planned Parenthood and the Right to Lifers, who, for some unknown reason, I thought should be right next to each other. By the time I was called to the scene, it was pretty ugly. Someone from Planned Parenthood was holding hostage the Right to Life's aborted fetus model. Using my high-level negotiating skills, I managed to rescue the hostage and move Planned Parenthood to the opposite end of the building, which seemed to calm the hostilities. But a riot was still brewing over:

1. The lack of traffic in the building
2. The lack of outside lights, thus making the area look deserted
3. The lack of air conditioning in a metal building when the outside temperature hovered at ninety degrees

It was hot in there in more ways than one.

As I was leaving what I called the Commercial Building, I heard a series of ominous booms. Actually, I felt them rather than heard them. The whole fairgrounds shook. My nerves were already somewhat frazzled by the vitriol spewing in the Commercial Building, and this potential catastrophe didn't help to alleviate that. I hurried back to the fair office to find that we were deluged with phone calls from irate neighbors. They wanted to know about the explosions and how many people were injured at the track event. The grandstand speaker kept broadcasting that there was "carnage everywhere" and that "bodies are flying." I sent my events director to the grandstand to see what the heck was going on as, by this time, I was hyperventilating and holding a paper bag to my face. It turned out that "the carnage" was all part of the show of blowing up a car, something I wasn't aware was going to happen. The event was supposed to be a "thrill show." I guess blowing up a car could be thrilling to the right group of people, which we apparently had at the fair that night.

The scent of gunpowder was still heavy in the air when I arrived at the fairgrounds the following morning. A very angry fire marshal, who didn't appreciate getting multiple phone calls from irate neighbors late into the night, was already waiting for me in my office.

"Gunpowder? Really? I had no idea," I pleaded, which was actually true. I used the "I'm new at this" card and got off with a warning, but also with the certainty that the fire marshal was going to inform the town supervisor of this travesty.

Bungee jumping was a fairly new fad in 1992, so we decided to have that "attraction" at the fair. Although it was located near the building that people seemed averse to entering (the one that housed a riot waiting to happen), the lack of lighting and distance from the midway didn't seem to deter those people who sought a near-death experience. There was always a healthy line of bungee jumpers. I could see the crane and the leapers from the window in my office. I have acrophobia. Just watching as they plunged into space made me physically ill. It wasn't as if there was a large air mattress to catch the jumpers if anything went wrong. There was only a four-foot-by-four-foot red Berber carpet on the asphalt. I suspect its purpose was to provide a target for a jumper should he find himself in free fall. The red color would camouflage the blood spatter. I closed the drapes in my office.

That year, we decided to have a kids' pet show. All kids and all animals were welcome. One of the livestock exhibitors (we'll call him Robby) decided he wanted to enter his fully grown Jersey cow in the show. The cow was a beauty with large, soft brown eyes and the amazingly long eyelashes that distinguish the breed. Robby put a rope around her neck and led her to the pet show tent that was probably a city block from the livestock building. The cow endured the indignity of being poked and prodded as well as the presence of the birds, snakes, cats, dogs, and gerbils until one of the dogs barked. She'd had enough. She pulled on the rope, dragging the hapless Robby several feet, and then bolted out of the tent and galloped down the midway. Without thinking, I took off after her until it occurred to me that the cow probably weighed a hundred and fifty times more than I did. Fortunately, the cow had a homing instinct and headed back to the barn on her own. Also, fortunately, it was raining, so there weren't many people (or reporters) on the fairgrounds for the cow to trample.

We had lots of entertainment that first year. My favorite was Oscar the Robot (pictured below). His handler, Jack, would stand somewhere close and have Oscar converse with the audience. It looked like Jack was smoking a cigarette (that was still okay in the 1990s), but the cigarette was actually a microphone that projected Jack's voice to the robot, making it appear that Oscar was speaking. The two frequently

took rest breaks in my office so that Oscar could literally recharge, and even though I knew Oscar wasn't a real person, I couldn't help talking to him. We were the first fair to employ the robot, and the attraction always remained a favorite of mine. Eventually, it became so popular that we could no longer book it, but every time Jack spotted me at another fair he was playing, he would call me over so that Oscar could "give me a hug."

The alligator wrestling show was another attraction that I was particularly fond of. The wrestlers were two young guys from Australia, or at least they spoke with a delightful Australian accent. They were pretty hunky, too. I also thought they were crazy. The alligators were huge with immense jaws, which explained the muscles on those guys (that I just happened to notice), which probably explains why the show was a favorite of mine.

We also had pig races. I eventually came to hate them, finding them boring and repetitious, but that first year, they were still a novelty. And despite my lack of enthusiasm for them in subsequent years, our audiences never seemed to tire of them, and they enjoyed the punny commentary of the ringmasters. The pigs had names like Elvis Pigsley, Kelvin Bacon, and Ham Solo, and they raced around a small track for their Oreo cookie rewards. Kids loved them and at least the races added to the agricultural element of the fair.

The Grange (also known as the Patrons of Husbandry) has always been the backbone of fairs. It was founded in 1867 when the country was largely agrarian, its purpose being "to advance methods of agriculture as well as to promote the social and economic needs of farmers in the United States."[2] The Grange became politically prominent, but as the country became more and more urbanized, it lost its political power. As fewer young people went into farming, it lost members, too, so that, at least in Monroe County, the Grange was primarily comprised of aging seniors, the average age probably being sixty-five. Nevertheless, the fair wouldn't have been complete without the Grange food booth. Unfortunately, the members didn't move too quickly, and remembering who ordered what was a challenge. There was always a large crowd around the Grange booth, not because the food was that good but because everyone was waiting for their orders to be ready. I do have to admit that their strawberry shortcakes were the best ever. The homemade biscuits were flaky and buttery, and the members picked the berries themselves. They were worth the wait.

And speaking of agriculture, people come to fairs expecting to see an array of farm animals. The year before I became fair manager, I think there were only three dairy cows entered in the fair and not a lot of other species. I began going to neighboring fairs and asking livestock exhibitors to come to Monroe County. I was told, "Nobody goes there. They don't appreciate us."

"I do," I protested, hating the whiny sound of my voice. So, I set out to woo them back. We moved the animals indoors to the air conditioned Minett Hall (I didn't tell the vendors who were sweltering in the Commercial Building, although I expect they knew), raised the premium money paid for showing, and put out the red carpet for exhibitors. (Actually, it was black rubber so the cows wouldn't slip on the concrete floor.) That first year, we had twenty-one cows. I would eventually grow the livestock barn to 171 cows and more sheep, goats, and rabbits than we could handle indoors. But that first year was a start. We were headed back to becoming an agricultural fair.

It was finally the last day of the fair. It had been an extremely hot week, and it had rained all day on Friday, but basically it had been okay. We were to close at 10 p.m. on Sunday, and by 9:45 p.m., I was finally relaxed enough to actually eat my first meal of the week. That's when two things happened: a fight in the Beer Tent, and a ride accident.

When there is a fight, one might think that bystanders would head in the opposite direction. Not true. Everyone flocks to the area to see what's going on. Even though I had security to handle the problem, as fair manager, I too headed in that direction. I quickly fought my way to the front of the crowd, planning how I would reason with the miscreants. I had never before seen anyone take a punch. I heard the crunch, saw the blood, and quickly revised my strategy. I turned and fought my way to the rear of the crowd and decided to investigate the ride accident instead, not that I could do anything there either.

The ride accident was on the Gravitron, a machine that uses centrifugal force to hold the rider in place as it spins. A boy of about seven had removed his harness and had subsequently gotten caught in one of the moving panels. The ride operator was able to release the boy, but the kid sustained a significant cut on his face. The operator was also hurt when he was thrown to the floor after pulling the boy out of the panel. Both went to the hospital by ambulance. I'm sure that my blood pressure was such that I should have been hospitalized too. This was my worst fear. As it turned out, both the child and the ride operator had only minor injuries. But it didn't stop the boy's parents from suing both the carnival and the fair, even though the ride operator said that the child had ignored his repeated warnings.

Anyway, the fight ended with a couple of bloody noses and black eyes, and with the two very inebriated participants taken into custody. And I never again allowed the Gravitron to be set up on the fairgrounds.

When all was said and done, despite the aforementioned incidents, my first fair was a success. We made money and attendance was up. I also lived through it. The fair board was happy and offered me a permanent position. Little did I know that my job at the fair would last for twenty years and that "The Rabbit Lady" would now come to be known as "The Fair Lady."

The Weather

"Whether the weather be fine. Whether the weather be not.
Whether the weather be cold. Whether the weather be hot.
We'll weather the weather, whatever the weather,
Whether we like it or not."

-old British tongue-twister

When it came to the fair, I obsessed about everything. The problem was that a fair takes on a life of its own, so I really had no control over anything. All I could do was roll with the punches, which is not a great option for a control freak. When there are hundreds of cows, sheep, goats, pigeons, and rabbits, anything can and usually does happen. One year on the night before the fair opened, I went to the livestock barn to find that some of the sheep had escaped from their pens and were busy investigating the building. It's a good thing I had just watched the movie *Babe* because the only people available to corral and get the critters re-confined were two flower show superintendents, a farm kid who hated sheep, and me. I pretended I was a sheep dog and ran around in circles, flapping my arms and making barking noises. It was not a pretty sight.

Not only were there hundreds of animals to contend with, along with their various uncivilized and unpredictable behaviors, but there were thousands of people, many of whom also had uncivilized and unpredictable behaviors. But the thing I worried about the most was THE GREATEST UNPREDICTABLE: the weather. And of course, it was the one thing that could make or break a fair.

I had good reason to worry about the weather. I lived in an area where the weather was volatile at best. A sunny day with no rain in the forecast would suddenly turn stormy. Since our bad weather usually came from the west, I constantly evaluated the skyscape in that direction. Were those thunder clouds? Why was the sky that sickly black and yellow color? Was it a tornado (I always went to the worst-case scenario) or just a bit of rain?

I wish I had been a fair manager in California. It never rains there in the summer. I could have put that worry to rest. In the twenty years I was a fair manager, there was only one year when it didn't rain, and that year it was a hundred degrees in the shade.

I became absolutely paranoid about the weather and think I may have actually been a conduit for rain. One year, we were in a severe drought. The only week it rained all spring and summer was fair week. I was told that farmers used to time their plantings to fair week because they always knew it would rain. This was not encouraging.

My paranoia came to a head one year in particular. Setup Day was perfect. There wasn't a cloud in the sky. Opening day of the fair was another story. A hurricane had come farther up the east coast than predicted, and we were getting the tail end of the rain. More rain fell on Monroe County on that one day than had ever previously been recorded. Roads were closed as creeks overflowed their banks while storm sewers struggled to keep up with the relentless precipitation, their waters turning underpasses into lakes. Some people ended up at the fairgrounds because they simply couldn't get home.

Shortly before the fair was scheduled to begin, I was standing in the beef cattle tent when the skies opened. Forget buckets. The rain came down in bushels. In no time, there was eight inches of water in the tent. I kept waiting for the rain to stop before I made my escape, but it never did.

I always tried to look my best on opening day, especially for the opening ceremony that the press covered. I really didn't want to go on TV looking like a drowned rat. But by the time I made it back to my office from the beef cattle tent, my hair hung in strings, the temporary brown rinse I had put in it that morning was running down my face in rivulets, my clothes were clinging to me like a second skin, and my brand new, white sneakers were covered in red clay. Fortunately, the press was busy with the storm so they didn't bother with the opening ceremony anyway.

That was the first day, and things went down the storm drain from there. The weather forecast changed by the minute, usually for the worse, as the storm stalled over our area. Each night, I prayed that the next day would dawn bright and shiny. Each morning, I woke up to rain and gloom. One morning, I was watching the weather on TV as I got dressed. The smiling weatherman said it was going to be a beautiful, sunny day. I looked out the window. It was raining. Perhaps it was a prerecorded weather report, or perhaps the weatherman was in some unknown, enchanted niche where it never rained until after sundown, like Camelot. He sure wasn't where I was.

But fair exhibitors are hardy souls. The beef cattle exhibitors built little dikes and moats to channel the water so the cattle could sit high and dry; the exhibitors wore boots or muddy sneakers that looked like mine. We made room for the sheep in the dairy cattle barn since the sheep tent was located in a low area of runoff that resembled Niagara Falls. All the animals stayed dry and happy while we mortals continued to brave the elements.

The biggest challenge was the grandstand. The first two rows of bleachers were under water. If a child fell off any of the other seats, he would need a life vest to keep from drowning. But the demolition derby drivers were game to compete anyway. So we rented a pump and began pumping water off the track. It was a clay track. If you have ever worked with clay, you know how sticky it gets when wet. I tried to walk on the track and sank up to my shins in the wet clay. Someone pulled me out, but one sneaker was sucked in. After pumping thousands of gallons of water, we finally had to call it quits and cancel the derby, much to the dismay of all the people who came to watch it despite the pouring rain. Go figure.

Of course, the weather during the weeks following that fair was perfect. I'd wake up every morning, see the sun shining, and pull the covers over my head. I was heard mumbling several times a day, "This would have made a perfect fair week." Of course the response, "You can't do anything about the weather, so stop beating yourself up," just caused me to beat myself up more.

But that wasn't the only year the weather was an issue. During my first fair, a great deal of rain came down in a very short period of time. The storm sewers simply couldn't handle that volume of water, so two things happened. First, geysers arose from the storm drains in the Dome and in the toilets in the men's bathroom—quite a surprise, I imagine, if you happened to be using the facilities at the time. Simultaneously, water filled up the midway area so that rides, foods, and games were under about ten inches of water. Once the rain stopped, nothing happened. The water just sat there.

Since it was late in the day on Friday, calling a plumber would have been a financial disaster. I had no choice. I had to call the town supervisor for help, which was not high on my list of fun activities. First of all, he didn't like having the fairgrounds in his town. Secondly, he didn't like me personally because I didn't live in his town. And thirdly, he didn't think I was capable of running the fairgrounds anyway, all of which he expressed to me on numerous occasions. Moreover, he had already heard from the fire marshal about my gunpowder transgression. To top it off, one of the students who was directing the parking for us had inadvertently parked cars over the property line and onto town property, causing damage to the grass in the form of muddy ruts. This, apparently, was my fault too, even though I had no idea it had happened.

I really didn't want to call Mr. Supervisor, but necessity breeds . . . necessity, so I made the call. He was not pleased to hear from me. But to his credit, he saw that I was up a creek without a paddle, quite literally, and he—not exactly graciously—agreed to send a crew. Also to his credit, he never sent us a bill for services rendered.

The crew traced the blockage to the middle of the track's infield. When they flushed the drain line, they found a drowned groundhog, one of the hundreds that had made his home in tunnels under the track. Once they removed his body from the pipe, water began to flow, and the show went on.

In 2006, we were doing some major renovation work at the fairgrounds, and construction wasn't nearly complete when it was time for the fair. We designed the fair around the construction and hoped for the best, which of course didn't happen. It rained, so one-third of the fairgrounds was under water, one-third was under construction, and the other third was alternately muddy or rocky.

Worse than mere rain were the pop-up thunderstorms that seemed to plague us. These were usually accompanied by high winds and dangerous lightning. We always made numerous announcements to get people out of tents and into buildings before the storms hit, but there were always a few intractable people who ignored us. During one such storm, a man insisted on staying in the clam tent. He sat on a metal chair that was not only in a puddle of water, but also next to a metal tent post that he decided to hold onto. This man was obviously not too bright. When I got the call over the radio that someone had been electrocuted in the clam tent, my blood ran cold. I asked the president of the board to come with me because I was sure the man was dead. Turns out he was fine—only a little tingly. We sent him to the hospital anyway.

Rain on Setup Day is a particularly nasty business. Staff has no choice but to remain outdoors. Placing vendors in their spots, running electricity to their booths, and solving the myriad last-minute problems that crop up when hundreds of people are all trying to get situated at once is always difficult—but when the rain is coming down in torrents, it's a nightmare. One particularly rainy year, my maintenance supervisor got all his staff yellow rain ponchos. They decided to put their two-way radios into their poncho pockets. It sounded like a good plan until the rain came down so hard that their pockets filled with water and shorted out all the radios. I then had to rent a whole new set of radios for the fair, and it cost a small fortune to get all the wet ones repaired.

Our parking lots were simply grassy fields. That is, they were grassy fields when they were dry—which was never during fair week. When wet, they turned into mud bogs or actually clay bogs, which is worse because water doesn't absorb into the clay. Since people liked to park close to the fair's entrance—despite the fact that the parking lot in that particular area was like quick sand (or quick clay)—we consistently had cars sink up to their hubcaps in the muck. We always had to have a tow truck handy to pull them out of it as well as a stash of fair passes to hand to the unhappy, and usually surly, car owners.

It's not just rain that can ruin a fair. Heat can be just as deadly. Since we held our fair in late July, I don't know why we continually expected that we would have moderate temperatures. It was always bloody awful. If the thermometer said ninety degrees, you can bet that on the blacktop it was 100. We finally started opening the fair at 4 p.m. on weekdays instead of in the mornings. The temperature was at least tolerable in the evenings, and we always got our best crowds starting around 6 p.m. However, the time change ruined our Senior Days as seniors tended to be up and about early and back home by dark. Of course, seniors also got free admission and seldom bought ride tickets, so the time change didn't hurt our bottom line, just our public relations.

CHAPTER FIVE

A Snapshot of America

I am a fair junkie. Wherever I go, I am constantly on the alert for the smell of sausage, peppers, and onions. Even when my family was on vacation in the Virgin Islands, I found the county fair. I can't help it. My heart pounds at the distant sight of the Sky Wheel. As it did when I was a kid, the music of a carousel draws me to it like a siren's song. I am also addicted to candy apples and have been known to drive for miles to find one that was made with just the "right" variety of apples and flavoring.

In my search for the perfect candy apple, I traveled to many fairs and found that they are truly, "snapshots of America." Once a year, people across the country pause in their everyday lives to reflect, to celebrate, and to showcase what has happened in their communities. These celebrations are living histories of all the elements that are unique to that region. While each fair has the same general components of competition, entertainment, agriculture, and midway, each fair is uniquely reflective of its own community.

I wish I could say that I thought up the phrase "a snapshot of America." It actually originated with my marketing director, but it resonated with me. From small agricultural centers to large urban settings, fairs provide a picture of that community's life at a given moment in time.

The word "fair" has its roots in the Latin word *feria*, which means feast day or holy day. An early mention of fairs is in the book of Ezekiel in the Bible, when fairs were of religious importance and often sources of revenue for churches. They spread throughout Europe during the Renaissance but gradually became social and commercial events rather than religious ones. As the New World was settled, a new kind of fair appeared. In 1811, the first American county fair was held in Pittsfield, Massachusetts when a farmer urged his neighbors to join him in a livestock show.[3] The purpose of those early fairs was for competition as farmers showcased their prime stock or newest hybrids to other farmers. It was also a place for farmers to see the latest agricultural technologies.

As the country changed from an agrarian society to a manufacturing one, fairs also changed. With only two percent of the population now farmers, most people became estranged from their sources of food and fiber. Fairs became places where non-farm people could see, touch, smell, and taste agriculture. They became opportunities for farmers to connect with consumers and to educate the urbanized public about the importance of agriculture in their everyday lives.

Unfortunately, it was difficult to convince our local farmers of that. They felt that fairs were for farmers, as they had been in the past, and for a long time, they totally missed the point that they were terrific marketing opportunities for them. The farmers complained about how uninformed the public was regarding pesticides and land usage, but they didn't see the potential for educating them through the county fair. Eventually, we established a relationship with the Farm Bureau, and they agreed to have an exhibit at the fair, but I wish I could have convinced them sooner to take advantage of the fair's educational mission instead of clinging to outdated paradigms.

One of their misconceptions was that the modern fair was "just a carnival" and that we should do away with the midway and return to a simpler agriculture-only event. However, carnivals have a long history and a place at fairs that actually started at the Chicago World's Fair (also known as the World's Columbian Exposition) in 1893. Buffalo Bill Cody desperately wanted to be part of that event with his Wild West Show, but the fair's organizer insisted that the cost of Cody's participation would be fifty percent of Cody's gross proceeds. That was totally unacceptable to the showman, so instead, he leased fifteen acres of land adjacent to the World's Fair site. He then opened his Wild West Show three weeks before the exposition opened, and over its seven-month run, his company performed for over five million people, often hosting more viewers than the exposition.[4] The synergy between the two events was recognized, and that was the start of what would become a partnership between fairs and carnivals. (Incidentally, the Ferris Wheel made its debut at the Chicago World's Fair as the fair's organizer wanted to outdo the spectacular Eiffel Tower that had been presented at the 1889 World's Fair in Paris.)

What the local farmers also didn't seem to understand was that carnivals are the hooks that get people to come to fairs so that they can then experience agriculture. "Come to the fair and see a goat" doesn't have quite the same appeal as "Come to the fair and thrill to the death-defying rides on the midway." Moreover, carnivals are financial necessities. At least twenty-five percent of a fair's revenue comes from carnivals that pay rent and ride commissions.

The successful fair has many elements, the carnival being one of them. When all of the elements come together, a unique event is created. It's called "edutainment." It gives people the opportunity to have fun while they learn. It also allows them to experience all that is good in their communities: the people, the businesses, and the agriculture.

Fairs really do take an annual snapshot of life and showcase a little slice of the America in which they are held. And the best part is that each fair has candy apples.

When a Good Idea is a Bad Idea

One year, I visited the New York State Fair where I saw the Native American Village (then called the Indian Village.) It was in an area set apart from the fair and was a real cultural center. People loved it.

Since we were always looking to attract new audiences to our fair, I had the brilliant idea of having a Heritage Village. Monroe County was home to many different ethnic groups who, like my family when I was growing up, never came to the fair.

My concept was simple. Have each group set up a food booth featuring its own cuisine. On the stage, we would rotate ethnic performances of song and dance. There was a wonderful area of the fairgrounds that was grassy and somewhat isolated (that being the key word), and I thought we could set up a separate "land" *a la* Disney. The community as a whole would be exposed to new cultures, and the various ethnic groups would advertise to their own and bring new people to the fair. It sounded like a good plan to me.

My staff and I went out into the community to connect with various cultural groups. Rochester had a big Puerto Rican population, and they were enthusiastic about the idea. We also contacted the Macedonian, the Jamaican, the Greek, the African-American, the Indian, and the Italian communities, all of whom had their own festivals in our county. We rented a stage, ran electricity to the area, brought in benches and tables, made all kinds of signs directing people to Heritage Village, and the vendors set up their food booths. The area was beautiful: a grassy oasis in the middle of the busy fair. There were Greek and Macedonian pastries, Italian ices, enchiladas, jerk chicken, and a whole host of other delectables. The stage had a full schedule of performers that included Macedonian folk dancers,

African drummers, and storytellers. What we didn't have were people to eat the food or to watch the entertainment. Try as we might, we could not get people to change their traffic patterns and walk over to the area.

The vendors who had angrily sweltered in the non-air conditioned metal building at my first fair, were tame compared with these people. I was summoned to the Village numerous times where I was threatened with law suits as well as assurances that the county executive would hear about my incompetence. But there was nothing I could do. I couldn't force people to go where they didn't want to go.

Live and learn, right? So what did we do? We did Heritage Village again at the next fair . . . to the same result. I still think it was a good idea.

The first year we did Heritage Village, we also decided to do paintball. The paintball arena was directly in front of where we put the Village. The only thing preventing paintballs from flying into the Village was the back of the stage, which was substantial, one of the two deciduous trees located on the fairgrounds, and stacks of hay bales that we had strategically placed. We thought we had it covered until I was standing in Heritage Village and felt something whiz past my ear. The bullets continued to come, repeatedly striking the Italian ice trailer that was directly in their path, and terrorizing the cowering-in-the-corner Italian woman who was staffing it. She threatened a lawsuit for emotional distress. I think she would have won her case.

There was one fair in particular that was probably the most stressful. It started when a promoter approached us about running a concert during the fair. He said he would arrange and pay for the talent and advertise and promote the concert in the Rochester area. We would give him the venue for free and get a percentage of on-site ticket sales as well as the bar income. It sounded like a dream come true because we didn't have the budget to bring in nationally known entertainment. The show was to consist of multiple acts with the headliner performing last. The only trouble was, although the promoter *advertised* the headliner, he never *actually booked* the headliner.

Came the night of the concert, and we were deluged with people. We could hardly keep up with ticket sales. The time came for the concert to start and nothing happened. The people were good sports and continued to drink and to eat fried chicken, purchased from the food booth of a locally popular vendor that was located directly in front of the concert venue. They waited and waited and waited. It was then that I learned that the headliner had never been booked and that the promoter had not paid the other performers, who were refusing to get out of their limos until they got their money. Meanwhile, the promoter was going around to ticket booths and snatching money, trying to come up with what he needed to get the entertainers out of their cars. The unsuspecting volunteers who staffed the booths didn't know the promoter from Adam. They thought they were being robbed.

It was nearly an hour after the concert was supposed to start, and the promoter was still running around, trying to amass enough money to get people out of their limos. If the concert didn't start soon, there were going to be a lot of very angry and very drunk people wanting refunds. I decided that I didn't have a choice. I had to advance the promoter $10,000 so the show could go on. I figured I'd lose my job if I didn't get the money back, but the alternative of facing an angry, drunken mob was worse. So I gave the promoter the cash, he paid the performers, and the show proceeded. Of course, the audience was waiting for the headliner, who we knew was a no-show. We prepared for the worst and alerted security. The show wrapped up, the announcement was made that the headliner was not going to appear, and, wonder of wonders, it started to rain. At that point, everyone left. It was the only time I was ever grateful for rain.

The next morning, the entire area in front of the Festival Tent was covered in chicken bones. It looked like a chicken massacre had occurred, and the maintenance crew had to figure out how to get piles of chicken bones out of the grass before we opened for the day.

Since the fair wasn't scheduled to start until noon, I decided to sleep in. I was emotionally and physically drained. I was sound asleep when I got a phone call from my frantic secretary, saying that the promoter was looking for me and that he had armed bodyguards with him. I quickly called my security chief and asked him to alert every member of my staff to show up within the hour for a meeting in my office. If the promoter wanted to show force, so would I.

We gathered in my office, the promoter with his armed security on one side of the table, me with my rent-a-cops on the other. I still had some of the ticket money, which the promoter wanted, but I was not about to release it until I got my $10,000 back. I insisted on cash. The promoter said he would write a check. I know I looked tired, but I don't think I looked stupid. I told the promoter he could write a check only if he came with me to the bank so that we could verify it was good and cash it on the spot. He reluctantly agreed.

We took off in a caravan of five cars, me riding with my marketing director. When we got to the bank, a small branch located in a strip mall, ten people descended, unannounced, on the tiny office of the unsuspecting branch manager. The bank manager knew me well and must have gathered from the deer in the headlights look on my face that I was distressed, so he agreed to expedite the check cashing. That's when I discovered that, somewhere between the fairgrounds and the bank, I had lost the check. Trying to be nonchalant as I searched through my purse, pockets, and briefcase, I whispered to my co-worker that I couldn't find the thing. He mumbled an excuse about needing to get something from his car and left me in the small office with the bank manager and eight very large, antsy men who had guns. I kept talking about nothing in particular as I tried to tamp down my panic. The bank manager simply looked perplexed. I'm sure it was only a few minutes, but it seemed like an hour before my cohort finally returned with the check that I had dropped on the floor of his car. Thankfully, the check was good, I paid the promoter money from ticket sales, and we all parted with sighs of relief, especially the bank manager.

Of course, the fall-out over not having the headliner came back to bite us, even though it wasn't our fault. We worked with that promoter one more time, not during the fair but with a separate concert event. He pulled a similar stunt, and I vowed never to work with him again.

Finally, it was Sunday of fair week. Like many other fairs, we'd decided to do a fundraiser we called The Great Cow Maneuver. One of our board members had devised a grid of the horse arena, and board members were supposed to sell plots on the grid. We'd then put a cow in the horse arena and wait for it to defecate. If the cow plopped on your plot, you'd win fifty percent of the take.

My marketing director and I went out to the horse arena to physically mark off the plots. We were both exhausted, this being the last day of the fair as well as two days after the concert fiasco. It was also a hundred degrees in the shade, and the horse arena was not in the shade. That's when we figured out that the grid was wrong. Trying to do geometry when your brain is having trouble adding two plus two was beyond our capabilities, so we decided to scrap the idea and return the money to the people who had bought plots. Fortunately, the board hadn't sold a lot of them anyway, so the Great Cow Maneuver, which we renamed the Great Cow Caper, wasn't as bad as it could have been. Most of the tickets had been purchased by me or by members of my family, so we just chalked it up as donations to the fair.

Then there was the year we asked a local skateboard company to do demonstrations. The company was run by a great group of young men who were enthusiastic but somewhat oblivious as to what was going on around them. By that time, we had decided to put commercial exhibitors and nonprofits into the air-conditioned Dome, but we were always looking for ways to get more people into that building, other than when it was raining. Putting the skateboarders there seemed like the perfect solution, so we set up a twenty-by-fifty foot arena that was delineated by two-and-a-half foot high blue pipe and drape.

Until that time, I didn't realize that skateboards could fly. I was at the first performance when a wayward flying skateboard flew by me and narrowly missed beaning an exhibitor. Skateboards rolled across aisles, under exhibit booths, and over the top of the pipe and drape. Exhibitors and fairgoers alike leaped and ducked for safety, sometimes both at the same time. I sent an S.O.S. over the radio to security and staff, and we formed a cordon around the demo area, trying to waylay the errant skateboards. When that first demo was over and no one had died, we re-grouped. We called every farm within fifteen miles of the fairgrounds and secured as many hay bales as we could, using them to make solid barriers around the perimeter of the demo area. Then we calmed the exhibitors and reined in the skateboarders. The next year, we put the skateboard demonstrations outside.

Still, getting people to come into the Dome was always a challenge. So we put a sign outside the Dome's entrance. It read:

FREE FUN

AIR CONDITIONED

REST ROOMS

That wasn't exactly the message we wanted to get across. It's a good thing we had bathroom attendants who constantly monitored the restrooms. No telling what kind of "free fun" people thought we had going on in them.

One year, we used "A Snapshot of America" as the theme for the fair. We lined the walls in the corridor that went from the Dome to the livestock barn (Minett Hall) with white paper and asked fair visitors to write their names and where they were from on the paper. We had some pretty interesting kids in the livestock barn that year, and they wrote a lot of colorful things on those papers that had nothing to do with geography. They strung obscenities together in ways never before seen. After replacing the paper three times within an hour, we finally abandoned the plan.

But the kids weren't finished. The livestock judging ring was filled with sawdust to provide a non-slip surface for the show animals. One morning, we went into the livestock barn to find that the kids had swept all the sawdust into the shape of a giant penis. I thought it was hilarious; the barn superintendents were not amused.

Extreme Band Mania was another great idea gone awry. We did auditions before the fair and judged numerous high school rock bands. Some were perfectly dreadful, some only moderately bad, and a few were on the good side of bad. We reasoned that the band members would bring people from their schools to the fair, so we planned "the finals" of the competition for Saturday night, our busiest time. Nobody came. The bands performed to empty seats, and everyone else complained about the awful music. I still have my Extreme Band Mania t-shirt as well as my Rockin' Country Blues Fest shirt—another one of our unsuccessful "good ideas."

Whenever I went anywhere with my grandchildren, they always had a little allowance money they could spend however they wanted. I thought that if we had a booth at the fair that sold inexpensive trinkets, we might make a little extra money. It was a year that the fair had a sports theme, so I ordered 1,000 soccer ball key rings, 1,000 basketball superballs, 500 Mardi Gras beads (for no particular reason), and twelve cases of snack chips. We decided to sell everything for $1 each. At the end of the fair, I still had 1,000 key rings, 990 superballs, 500 Mardi Gras beads, and eleven cases of chips. We gave away the chips to the Senior Bingo for Fun and Prizes players and people in the Beer Tent, but we still had a lot of chips leftover that eventually got stale. I put them out at board meetings anyway (a bit of passive-aggressiveness on my part.) As for the trinkets, we found uses for them, but it took ten years to get rid of them all.

The problem was that I couldn't say no to anything. I have always been the champion of lost causes and hopeless cases, so, if an idea sounded like a good one, I'd of course say, "Let's try it." But if an idea sounded iffy, I'd still say, "Let's try it and see if it works." And if an idea sounded like there was no way in hell it would succeed, it was inevitable that I'd nonetheless say, "Let's try it and see if we can make it work." As a result, I spent a lot of time trying to get people to go somewhere and to do something in which they had no interest.

I still say that my ideas had merit. Maybe I just needed a more compliant audience.

CHAPTER SEVEN
When a Good Idea is a Good Idea

Over the years, I had many great ideas that remained great only in my own mind. I found it impossible to predict which project would be a disaster and which would soar, and I became quite adept at whining and gnashing my teeth. It got hard to think positively, and I was sure that if I did, the gods were waiting to smite me for my arrogance. It was easier to expect the worst and be surprised when things went well than to be disappointed when a sure "hit" became a "huh, what happened?" event. But then lightning struck and we had several remarkable successes that completely astounded me.

Although there now seems to be a resurgence of interest in the homely arts, in the 1990s, many of those skills seemed to be fading from existence. I'm talking about things like embroidery, crocheting, sewing, quilting, and even baking. We were constantly beating the bushes for exhibitors for our Home Arts Department so that we would have a lot of items to put on display. I decided to form a home arts committee, hoping that an influx of new people would produce innovative ideas on how to enhance the department. The committee worked out better than I thought possible, especially when they came up with the idea of having an annual community service project.

That first year, we advertised to knitting and sewing guilds that we needed lap robes to donate to Unity Hospital for its outreach and dialysis programs. We sent out a press release in January so that people would have an opportunity to complete their projects by the July fair. Within a month, the lap robes started coming. And they just kept coming. We got over a thousand lap robes from senior centers; youth groups; sewing, knitting, and crocheting guilds; university women's clubs; and individuals just looking for projects to keep them busy over the long winter months. It took ten people a week to hang all the lap robes so that they could be on display at the fair. The hospital coordinator, who came to the fair expecting to take a couple of boxes of lap robes back in the trunk of her car, was in a state of shock. She needed to send a truck! I wouldn't be surprised if the hospital still has a few boxes of lap robes tucked away somewhere.

Every year, we did a different project. One year it was winter scarves, another, mittens and hats. And every year, the outpouring from the community exceeded our expectations. The Home Arts Department looked great and full of exhibits, and we made a difference for a lot of people.

Since education is a big part of the fair's mission, the home arts committee also decided to do some outreach at non-fair time, hoping the extra exposure would attract new audiences and encourage more people to enter their projects in the fair's competitions. We teamed up with Cornell Cooperative Extension, which already had a trusted name in the community, and did several cooking classes that proved quite successful. The theory was simple. Provide an educational event, make it free, and be sure to advertise that the participants got to eat whatever was prepared, the latter being key, especially as far as seniors are concerned. Our workshops included pie making, bread baking, growing and cooking with herbs, growing and cooking with strawberries, and our most popular, a workshop on making tea correctly, including using a heated teapot, and how to make scones—a somewhat tricky operation. This workshop turned into a giant tea party with attendees sampling different kinds of teas and both sweet and savory scones, all served on fine, bone china.

The workshop concept worked exceedingly well with more people entering our fair's home arts competitions every year. The spring we had our tea and scones party, so many people entered their scones in the food department that we had to add a whole new section to the Exhibitor's Handbook (the catalogue that described all the contests people could enter at the fair—from cookies to cows.) Not only did our home arts exhibits grow, but once the new exhibitors saw all the different competitions that the fair offered, we got an increase in the flower and vegetable, photography, woodworking, and collections departments. The workshop idea was another spectacular win for the fabulous home arts committee.

Having worked at 4-H and having had three kids who went through the 4-H program, I was a pretty strong supporter of youth development organizations. I didn't see why the fair couldn't sponsor a youth group. So I worked with the City of Rochester's Youth Bureau, and we started a youth group that was called Youth Taking Action. This group consisted mainly of urban teens who were learning how to become productive members of boards and committees. The only reason it worked was because of their coordinator. The kids had no transportation, so getting to and from the fairgrounds for meetings wouldn't have been possible if she hadn't made it a priority, no matter what time of the day or night the meetings were scheduled. She was a wonderful asset to the Youth Bureau, and she positively affected the lives of a lot of kids.

At our first meeting, one of the teen boys sat slumped in his chair, his eyes half-closed. He never said a word. I thought, "Oh, boy. This kid doesn't want to be here. Do the others? This is going to be a fiasco." It turned out that he was simply tired as he had just finished spearheading another event. He was a natural leader and speaker and the prime mover of the club for several years. Rochesterians are now quite familiar with him as he recently won the Democratic primary and will most likely be the next mayor of Rochester. Malik Evans was a most impressive teen, and he has become an even more impressive adult as he tackles increasingly difficult leadership challenges.

The kids decided that the way to reach other teens was through their talent. They began building a step dance program, which consisted of team dance performances involving stomping, clapping, and synchronized movement. Step dancing became very popular in urban schools and eventually led to the establishment of a county-wide competition. We had step competitions, not only at the fair, but also as stand-alone performances. The kids planned, organized, and ran the events, and I just stood back and provided support. I was so proud of those kids and proud that they included me in their successes.

Fairs are supposed to support youth and agriculture. We decided to do both at once and have an Agricultural Education (Ag Ed) Center that would provide hands-on activities for kids so they could really experience agriculture. One of my board members took on the project. She traveled to many parts of the state, gathering educational materials from Cornell University and the Geneva Experimental Station. The kids loved the exhibit, and many parents said it was the highlight of the fair.

The first year of the Ag Ed Center, we had a setback. The coordinator had ordered a thousand ladybugs from a supplier and planned on giving a ladybug to each of the kids in support of the integrated pest management station in her exhibit. Unfortunately, when she opened the box of ladybugs, she found that they all had died in transit. Undaunted, she played up one of the other stations, which turned out to be the one the kids liked the best. The station featured a black light. She first asked the kids to wash their hands. Then she shined the black light on those supposedly clean hands so the kids could see all the dirt that was left behind. It freaked them out.

When the kids completed all the stations, they were each given a piece of cheese, billed as a healthy snack, to take with them. The cheese had been donated by a local cheese processor, but the company sent us so much that we ended up distributing cheese to the seniors who were playing at the Senior Bingo for Fun and Prizes activity. That was a big hit. Then we started handing out cheese as people left the fair. I think the cheese was multiplying because, when the fair was over, we still had cartons of it.

My board member not only designed the Agricultural Education Center, but she also set it up and staffed it for every hour of every day of the fair. That's quite a feat when you figure that the outside temperature averaged ninety degrees and that she was located in a tent in full sun. Fair people are extraordinary. That year at the New York State fairs' convention, we won the Agricultural Awareness

Award for that exhibit.

Senior Bingo for Fun and Prizes was another idea that worked well. We had all the right elements: it was free, there were prizes, and there was free food. Those are all "must haves" in order for our senior citizens to participate. But we did learn a valuable lesson the first year we did the event. We needed to hide the food and to serve it piecemeal because seniors were walking away with whole boxes of cookies stuffed into their purses or under their shirts. (I wish they had walked away with more of the cheese.) Every year, a man from the Henrietta Senior Center was our bingo caller. When he began this activity, he was well into his 80s. We were never sure from year to year whether he would be with us again, but he never let us down.

Spaceport was another good idea that worked well in some respects but not well in others. At the time, Monroe County was the headquarters of technological giants Eastman Kodak, Xerox, and Bausch and Lomb. The area was also home to five colleges, including the Rochester Institute of Technology and the University of Rochester. The people involved in those businesses and institutions comprised a major segment of the region's work force, and they had a keen interest in science and in new technologies. We thought we could attract an untapped audience to the fair if we were to bring in exhibits that showcased space technology. We turned to NASA for ideas.

At the 1996 Olympics in Atlanta, NASA had an exhibit that consisted of two, full-scale mockups of pods from the International Space Station. People had flocked to the exhibit and had lined up for blocks to see it. We arranged with NASA to get it.

The exhibit was free, except that shipping it cost $15,000. I managed to squeeze the cost into my fair budget, and we eagerly awaited the exhibit's arrival. The set-up instructions we got in advance were very specific. The trailers had to be put on perfectly even ground. No place on the fairgrounds even approached that specification. We revised our fair lay-out and finally settled on an area that was the flattest we could manage, even though it was out of the traffic pattern of the fair. Knowing what we did about getting people to go where we wanted them to go rather than where they wanted to go, we were fearful that this might be a disaster. Still, people had lined up in Atlanta, so we had hope, and we were afraid NASA would refuse to allow the trailers to stay if we didn't meet their specifications.

Finally, the trailers arrived along with two people from NASA who would set them up and staff the exhibit during fair hours. That's when we learned that the trailers had leveling devices, so we could have placed them anywhere. By that time, everything else was set, so it was too late to move them to another location. We also learned that we needed to feed and house the two people from NASA, so we begged local hotels and fast food restaurants, as well as some fair food concessionaires, for free stuff. I don't think the two men were used to eating fair food or having Burger King meals, but they didn't complain, and I think they had fun that week anyway. One night, I treated the two to a "garbage plate," a Rochester specialty that consists of two hot dogs (or two hamburgers), baked beans, macaroni salad (or home fries), piled together and topped with onions, mustard, and a spicy hot meat sauce. I hate to say it, because Rochester prides itself on this concoction, but the men from NASA were not impressed.

The exhibit itself was spectacular. It gave people a really good idea of our astronauts' living quarters in the space station. It even addressed the question that every kid wanted to know: how do you go to the bathroom in space?

We advertised the heck out of the space station, and when the fair opened, we expected the kind of crowds that had appeared in Atlanta. It didn't happen. Although we had a steady flow of people who viewed it, we never had numbers that justified the $15,000 expenditure. Also, I'm sure that its location on the fairgrounds didn't put the exhibit front and center as we had wanted. But something good did happen. We were approached by members of the New Frontier Society, a local branch of the National Space Society, about becoming involved in future fairs. That was the beginning of a yearly exhibit we called Spaceport that we housed in the Dome.

We found that NASA had a lot of exhibits we could get that were free of charge, including shipping, and over the next few years, we had some great stuff, from rocket models, to hydroponics displays, to a virtual reality theater. The members of the New Frontier Society staffed Spaceport, and they had impressive informational kiosks that supplemented the items from NASA. We even started doing a reception in Spaceport, complete with dress-up characters. We served green apple punch, cheese in the shape of stars and moons, and cookies, using Klingon names for all our goodies. (Although the reception was supposed to last an hour, it usually survived for only about twenty minutes as hordes of seniors and kids descended on the free food.)

One of the things we really wanted to do was get an astronaut to come to the fair. Every year, we applied to NASA, but we never got very far as the requirements for astronaut appearances were difficult for us to meet. Finally, we had all of the parameters in place, and it looked as if we were going to get Buzz Aldrin, who was president of the National Space Society, to come. We were so certain that we were on his agenda that I started referring to him as "Buzz." Then Alan Shepherd died, and all the astronauts went to his funeral. That was that.

Nevertheless, the alliance between the fair and the New Frontier Society was a good one. The members were enthusiastic volunteers, and the displays added a new dimension to the fair. Still, we never saw an influx of new people coming to the fair specifically for this technology. That always puzzled me, but it didn't stop me from constantly looking for "the WOW factor" to present each year. The exhibits from NASA were definitely WOW inspiring. Moreover, they taught me something I didn't expect.

While searching for partnerships for our first NASA exhibit, I went to a company called Infotonics to explore the possibility of getting a sponsorship to help offset the shipping costs. Infotonics was a nonprofit corporation that developed ideas for entrepreneurs using products that relied on microchip technology. If that sentence doesn't mean much to you, join the crowd. I didn't have a clue what it meant.

I never questioned how my cell phone worked, or how telephone calls were switched all over the country, or actually, how anything worked. They just did.

Going to Infotonics was a humbling experience. It made me realize that there was a whole world out there that I knew nothing about. Worse yet, I didn't even realize that I knew nothing about it. It was mind boggling to learn about some of the fantastic products that were in development, using technology that seemed like science fiction to me. The products were affecting my life on a day-to-day basis, yet I was totally ignorant about the whole concept upon which they were built. I felt as if I had been living in a cave for fifty years.

That got me thinking about fairs and their traditional role of educating people like me about the newest technologies, whether they were agricultural, space-related, manufacturing processes, or scientific advancements. While I was still in the Dark Ages when it came to physics, other people in the community were in the dark about agriculture, or food safety, or space technology, or growing flowers, or quilting, or making pies. Fairs teach. Fairs showcase new stuff. Fairs open the doors to knowledge so that people can see, touch, and hear all those things that their lifestyles don't ordinarily allow them to see, touch, and hear. I also got to thinking about kids and how excited they might be about learning if they could feel the wonder that I felt after my tour of Infotonics. Maybe we didn't have the crowds of people I had envisioned who viewed our NASA exhibits, but I bet a lot of people had a new world opened to them, much as I had.

And speaking of "worlds," I found great inspiration for the fair business at Disney World, where my family and I visited a number of times. I really liked the on-site performances that spontaneously sprang up in various places around the parks. In talks with my marketing director, we thought that if we could develop such a group of performers, we could also use them as fair promotional tools by sending them to parades and various fairs and festivals throughout the area. Thus was born The Fair Kids.

We contacted a local dance instructor who had a troop that

consisted of eight teenage girls and one boy. She thought they would work well for us. She devised several dance routines, and she already had costumes, so we put the kids to work. They were an enthusiastic group, and they never shied away from a performance. When they were at their best, they were wonderful—acrobatic and in step. The rest of the time, their movements were not quite in sync, but they were charming and willing ambassadors for the fair, and we used them for about three years. I can never hear the song "Boogie Woogie Bugle Boy" without thinking fondly of them.

Perhaps the best thing that happened during the fair was something that was not my idea. In fact I gave strict instructions that it was not to happen. But as usual, my children didn't listen. In 2009 my grandson, Evan, was born on the Saturday of fair week, our busiest day. My son and his wife, who were both essential fair workers, left for an obstetrician's appointment at noon on Friday and never returned. My grandson was born the following morning. For years afterward, he was convinced that we held the fair in honor of his birthday.

When Evan was born, I did something I had never done before. I actually left the fairgrounds so that I could go to the hospital to hold him. It was the best two hours of my week.

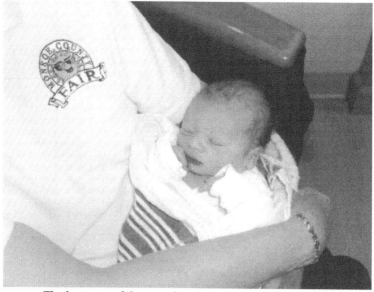

The best part of the 2009 fair—my grandson Evan's birth.

CHAPTER EIGHT

As the Wheel Turns
(Getting Organized)

Despite popular opinion, a fair is not put together in a few weeks. It takes a year to plan and organize. In fact, the planning of the next year's fair starts immediately at the conclusion of the previous one—or as soon as the staff is coherent again. Then it is critiqued— the staff and board decide what went well and what could be done better.

Most people say that I am an extremely well-organized person. What they don't know is that it is a self-preservation technique. I simply can't function in chaos. When I was in charge of an event the size and scope of the fair, it was essential for me to be totally organized before the chaos that is inherent in such an event actually hit. My philosophy was to plan, plan, plan, and then to organize everything I had planned so that when the pandemonium struck, I could focus on whatever challenges then ensued. That meant a heck of a lot of meetings.

I had many, many committees. Not only did I have a board of twenty-five members that met monthly, but I also had a fair committee, a finance committee, a personnel committee, a long-range planning committee, a buildings and grounds committee, a by-laws committee, a development/membership committee, a marketing committee, a technology committee, a nominating committee, and a youth committee. There were also sub-committees of the fair committee including the flower show committee, the livestock committee, the foods committee, the horse committee, and the home arts committee. On top of that, there were New Frontier Society meetings for Spaceport, school bus demolition derby meetings for the grandstand, Youth Taking Action meetings, and staff meetings. You may think that I spent most of my days in meetings. Not true. I spent most of my nights in meetings. In fact, my average work week was 55-60 hours, and I seldom got home before 9 p.m.

Some of our most productive meetings were our non-meetings. About once a month, I would go to our reception area to carry on a casual conversation with my secretary. Before long, someone else would join us and eventually, the whole office staff would show up. We'd talk and laugh and brainstorm, but most importantly, bond as a team. A number of our best ideas came out of those impromptu meetings.

But there were definitely other staff meetings that were conducted more formally. Each January, I called a staff meeting where we identified areas of the fair that needed to be addressed, starting with the opening ceremony and ending with the final day's grandstand event. Ticket sellers and takers, bathroom cleaners, pull tab sellers, youth day promotions, advertising, parkers, equipment rentals, senior bingo, grandstand events, entertainment for the stages, talent shows, and information booth materials and workers were just of few of the areas that needed leadership. We assigned a staff person to be in charge of each area. Since our key staff was only five people, each of us had multiple responsibilities.

As we got close to fair time, the meetings increased and got longer and more intense. Two weeks before the fair, we closed the office and did a day-long retreat. At that meeting, we went over every detail of the fair on an hour-by-hour basis, discussing what resources we needed, who was responsible for what, what problems we might encounter, and what additional help might be required. By the end of that meeting, everyone knew what his job was and how he would execute it.

A week before the fair, I held a security meeting. This included representatives from the New York State Police, the Monroe County Sheriff's Department, the ambulance company, the town's fire marshal, the Henrietta fire chief, and the head of our contracted security company. Again, we went over the fair day-by-day, fleshing out when we might have traffic control or security issues. We relied on the police to give us scuttlebutt concerning any gang-related activity so that we could be prepared and on the lookout for gang colors and clothing. And we made sure that the ambulance company was aware of horse shows, grandstand events, and senior and youth days that might require close monitoring. As a result, in my twenty years at the fair, we had only minor security issues.

Every morning before the fair opened, we held a meeting that included key staff, the maintenance supervisor, the head of our contracted security company, and a representative from the carnival. We would discuss problems we had encountered the day before, how to make sure they weren't repeated, and what to expect for the upcoming day. The carnival rep always brought donuts to the meeting, which was greatly appreciated as most of us never had time for breakfast.

You may think that having so many meetings was overkill, but our days started at 8 a.m. and didn't end until midnight or 1 a.m. Whether we had problems or not, the fair continued, and we had to be ready to move from one thing to the next without hesitation. When I asked some of my staff for their recollection of things that had happened at various fairs, they had only vague memories. Everything moved quickly, so details were easily forgotten as we transitioned from event to event.

Once the fair started and I got the opening ceremony out of the way, I really didn't have any particular responsibility. Pretty good planning on my part, I'd say. Actually, I had to be available to go where I was needed: as an extra hand at a ticket booth, to solve a problem, to handle a complaint, to interface with the carnival, to respond to a medical call, or just to make exhibitors or customers feel welcomed and appreciated. I had no particular responsibility, but I was ultimately responsible for everything. My staff never let me down, and although they didn't make my job easy, they made it doable.

One of the plans we had that worked extraordinarily well was our lost child plan. Frantic parents were directed to the office where we would get a full description of the child, including what he/she was wearing. Then the description would go out over the radio, and all staff members would stop what they were doing, if possible, and look for the lost child. That included gate people, security, maintenance, office staff, parkers, and the carnival. We cautioned parents to remain in the office while we looked. If they insisted on searching instead of waiting, we told them to return to the office if they found the child so that we wouldn't keep at it. We assured them that if they failed to do this, we would call them at 2 a.m. to check. That was a highly effective threat.

We usually found children within five minutes of when the alert was sent. We were very good at it, except for once. We looked for one child for about an hour with no success. We were getting a bit frantic when the child showed up in the office, saying he was lost. The boy bore absolutely no resemblance to the one for whom we were searching, including the clothes he was wearing. It turned out that he was the nephew of the women who had reported him lost. He had arrived the night before from New York City to spend a few weeks with her. She hadn't seen him in years and hadn't more than a vague idea of how he looked or what he was wearing. I saw the woman at the fair every year after that. She usually had five or six kids with her, and I always wondered if she knew who they were.

I remember one little boy who was brought to the office by security. He wasn't with an adult and had been in hand-to-hand combat with another child. We kept the boy in the office until his parents showed up. We told his mother that he had been fighting, at which point, she began spanking him while screaming, "We don't hit. We don't hit." I guess that's what you call "leading from behind."

Another plan that I developed was an emergency response plan that covered everything from fire in one of the buildings to guns on the fairgrounds to bomb threats. That plan went out to all law enforcement and governmental officials and to the carnival as well as to each member of my staff. It was comprehensive, and except for the lost child section, we, thankfully, never had to implement any of the incident sections. However, we did implement the preventive section that dealt with the management of E. coli contamination in animal areas.

Following a tragedy at the Washington County Fair when E. coli (Escherichia coli) bacteria accidentally entered the water supply, fair insurance carriers became extremely paranoid about the liability they were facing from E. coli exposure. Our insurance carrier sent me to a seminar in Kansas City so that I could learn what fairs needed to do to be protected from negligence law suits. I have to admit that the seminar scared the hell out of me.

E. coli bacteria, which can be present in the feces of livestock, can remain viable for long periods of time. It can live on fencing around livestock areas and on floors and walls in barns. The bacteria can be carried into cars and homes on a person's shoes or on the wheels of baby strollers. Baby bottles or pacifiers that are dropped in contaminated livestock areas can infect children and infants, who are especially susceptible to E. coli.

After learning all this, I felt it imperative that I not only protect the fair but that I do everything in my power to protect the public as well. The document that I prepared was a detailed plan on disinfection techniques and protocols for animal handlers and the public. It was a great plan, but after I wrote it, the implementation of it took many people many hours of work. Just putting up signs warning the public of the possible hazard took me an entire day. My signs told people that they needed to wash their hands after exposure to the animals, why they needed to wash their hands after exposure to the animals, and how they needed to wash their hands after exposure to the animals. Some were in English and some in Spanish, and they were at every bathroom and hand washing station, in multiple locations inside and outside every building that housed animals, at the horse arena, and at the admission gates. I admit that I was a little obsessive about it, but I don't think anyone could possibly argue that we didn't make the public aware of the potential problem.

The most labor-intensive part of the plan was the section on the total disinfection of the livestock barn following the fair so that it would be ready for subsequent shows. My maintenance staff was exhausted by the end of the fair, but they still had to clean out all the manure, wood shavings, and hay from the barn and then power-wash everything with disinfectant, from the ceiling beams to the floors. I was not popular with the maintenance staff during that procedure.

Another practice we put in place wasn't part of my emergency plan but came about as a result of an anonymous phone call. The caller maintained that our ticket sellers and takers were scamming tickets. We thought we had a pretty good accounting system that would prevent this, but just to be certain, we decided that every night when the ticket box was brought into the office at the close of the fair, we would manually count the tickets and put them in numerical order so that we could ascertain if there were out of sequence tickets that might indicate a problem. This was quite an undertaking. It wasn't so bad on days when the fair wasn't busy and the ripped tickets were few, but on the weekends, when the ticket box was dumped, the tickets took up the whole of the conference table. Still, we all pitched in. We were exhausted and usually pretty loopy by that time of night, so we weren't very efficient, but we laughed a lot, ate junk food (blooming onions were the favorites), and generally unwound from the rigors of the day. We never found any discrepancies, but we felt we were doing our due diligence.

CHAPTER NINE

The Grandstand

The grandstand was our bread and butter. If the grandstand was dark, our attendance suffered, so we aimed to have something booked for every night. We tried lots of different kinds of events. Things that worked well at many fairs did not work at ours. For example, tractor pulls are the staples for most fairs. At them, farm or modified tractors pull weighted "sleds." The tractor that pulls the greatest weight wins the heat. At the Hemlock Fair, which was held in a rural area just twenty miles down the road from us, the tractor pulls were always sell-outs. We tried them in our highly urban and suburban population; we had about five people watching.

We also tried mud bogs, stock car football, monster truck shows, motocross, garden tractor pulls, auto thrill shows (of the exploding car fame), sprint car races, and even ostrich races, but nothing drew the crowds like demolition derbies, where cars smashed into each other until there was only one car still running. We did best if we used the derbies as anchors on our opening and closing days. This forced people to the fair on days that would normally be sparsely attended and gave us the ability to book something less expensive on Saturday, our busiest day. The grandstands were always full on derby nights, and when the heats were over, people flooded the midway, riding the rides, buying food, and drinking beer: all components of a successful fair. That's why rain on derby nights was something to fear. If the derbies didn't go on, it really affected our bottom line.

Fortunately, our storms generally were over by nightfall. In the summer, heat built throughout the day, causing thunderstorms in the late afternoons and early evenings. Then, the skies cleared, and we had beautiful nights. But the rain wreaked havoc on the track, and the arena needed to be worked over and over with heavy equipment in order to dry out the mud and restore it to a usable condition. This always caused the derbies to start late, which was a pet peeve of mine.

After the derbies were over, there invariably would be fights between the derby drivers and the wrecking company in charge of taking away the destroyed cars. The rules stated that any cars left an hour following the derby would become the property of the wrecking company. With the high price of scrap metal, the derby drivers always wanted to take their cars back, but some of them traditionally entered multiple cars, so they had a problem getting them all off the track with-in the hour timeframe. The wrecking company saw dollar signs, so they were sticklers about the rule. As a result, fists would start to fly, and pretty soon, we'd have an all-out brawl on our hands until someone called for the police to step into the fray. When a man from the wrecking crew actually chased someone with a forklift, we "called time." We changed the rules so that, after the derbies, the cars belonged to the fair. Drivers had until the next morning to claim their cars, and we never gave anyone a hard time if they were late. We found a salvage company whose owners agreed to collect the cars the morning after the derbies, and the company split the income from the scrap metal salvage with us. Problem solved.

We were always on the lookout for an event that would entice people to the fair, not only on Saturdays but on our "off days" as well. It seemed that no matter what we tried, the results were mediocre at best. One year, a promoter held a motocross event the day before the fair, and the grandstand was packed. The next year, we tried motocross on opening day, and there were fewer than one hundred people in the stands. It made no sense. But then I had one of my brilliant ideas that actually worked.

It came to my attention that a fair in the Midwest was doing school bus demolition derbies. I figured that since car demolition derbies were so popular, bus derbies ought to hit just the right note with our audience. I ran the idea by the fair committee, and they agreed to give it a try. Their only stipulation was that we paint the buses some color other than school bus yellow so that kids wouldn't be traumatized by seeing school buses smashed. I thought the kids would actually *like* to see school buses smashed, but I was overruled.

I went on a search for school buses and found seven of them that a local church-school was selling for $300 each. I then had another (brilliant) idea of contacting some of the surrounding towns' volunteer fire departments to see if they might be interested in sponsoring and driving the buses. They jumped at the chance, and over the years, a friendly rivalry sprang up among the fire companies to see which one would take home the trophy. They became so creative in decorating their buses that we had to start a competition for the best-decorated bus as well as for the winner of the demolition contest. The firefighters took their decorated buses to parades, did TV interviews, and got their constituents to come to the fair to support them. Moreover, the public loved the event, from preschoolers to grandparents. It was a winner.

The firefighters always tried to decorate their buses to reflect the fair's theme for the year. After 9/11, our theme was "A Snapshot of America," and the buses were painted red, white, and blue, or army camouflage. I can't remember what the theme was for the year a bus was designed as a Dalmatian. The dog had a leg that could be lifted hydraulically, at which point water would squirt out as if the dog were peeing. The audience went wild.

As popular as the bus derbies were, I could never actually watch them. I got to know the firefighters personally, and I was always worried (because that's what I did) that someone would be seriously hurt. I went to the parade of buses before the derby but could never stay for the matches. I'd start to feel dread in the pit of my stomach and make a bee-line for the exit before the event started.

In truth, the buses were very safe. Their centers of gravity were such that tipping them over was extremely difficult. In all our years of competition, it happened only once. The driver emerged unscathed, and the crowd roared with approval. Still, every season, with input from the drivers, we modified the rules to make the event even safer, but I still could never make myself witness it.

Bus demolition derby, a crowd pleaser

What's left after the derby

The success of the event became well-known, and several other fairs began having bus derbies. After about seven years, it became very difficult to find buses. Whenever my husband and I drove anywhere,

I was constantly on the search for them, and more than once, I made him stop so I could approach a homeowner to see if the bus in his or her yard was for sale. I got quite good at spotting those yellow monsters, but finally, we simply couldn't locate any. The people at the salvage yard told me that buses were being bought up and taken to Mexico where they were being used for housing, an admittedly better use for them. We finally had to abandon the bus derby, much to the sadness of the firefighters and to our audiences.

Another successful event was our sprint car races. One of my board members was a racer and had an "in" at the local track. He encouraged us to do this event when our new track was built in the meadow. We had lots of participants who loved the track, but we had only mediocre attendance at the races. However, the event made money because of the entry fees for participants, so we did the races for several years despite the lack of sell-outs in the stands.

One year, my board member asked me if I would like to take a ride around the track during a lull between races. I thought that sounded like fun, so I agreed. He came to get me when it was time, and I figured it was no big deal. But the first thing he did was put me in a fire suit. I began to get nervous. Then he strapped me into the car. The seat was very narrow, and I was squeezed into it with the harness holding me immobile. Finally, he put a helmet over my head and face. That's when my heart started to pound, and I had trouble breathing. Did I mention that I am somewhat claustrophobic?

"How fast are we going to go?" I asked, the sound of my voice muffled by the helmet.

"Oh, fifty or sixty miles per hour," the driver replied nonchalantly.

That's when I learned that it wasn't a simple leisurely ride around the track during intermission. I was in the pace car for the next race. That was enough for me, and I started ripping off my helmet and pleading that I needed to get out of the car. After I made it back to safety, I found out that my staff had actually been taking bets on whether or not I'd go through with it. Bastards!

Preparing the track for motorsport events was always a long production, sometimes taking weeks. Also, with multiple events that were often vastly different from one another, modifications to the slope and dimensions of the track sometimes had to be done on a daily basis during the fair. I had two wonderful male volunteers who were always champing at the bit to use the heavy machinery and to work on the track. I loved them both; they actively disliked each other. I always felt that my job was to get the best out of people and to ignore their quirks, but being a constant referee was exhausting. I even tried dividing the days so that one would be in charge on one day and the other on another. Nothing worked, and I spent a lot of time begging each of them not to leave because I truly needed them both. I wish I could say that I found a solution to that problem, but I never did. I just hope they realized how much I valued each of them.

One of the problems we had at the new track had to do with fencing. Once we renovated and reconfigured the fairgrounds, we found that it was way too expensive to fence the entire perimeter. An area that remained open was on the far side of the track in what remained of the meadow. On the other side of the meadow was the Henrietta Town Park. We were alerted that people were going to the park, walking across the meadow, and getting into the fair for free. We watched for a while and saw that there was a steady stream of people who casually waved to us as they availed themselves of this opportunity. Still, the cost of hiring a security guard to police the area would not have been offset by the admission money collected. We decided that the people were probably spending money on rides and foods once they got into the fair anyway, so we let it go.

One year, we simply couldn't find an event for the grandstand on one of our weekdays. The Delaware County Fair always had a bike giveaway, and it was tremendously popular, so we thought we would try it. We got a bike shop to donate a couple of bikes, and we decided to do a scavenger hunt for kids in the track area before we did a drawing for the bikes. The event was free, and we divided the kids by sex and age groups. We prepared bags of goodies, and then let the kids onto the track where they searched for the bags, kind of like an Easter egg hunt.

Because the track was so dusty, we needed to put the goodies into plastic bags. We used the superballs, beads, and keychains that were left over from the unsuccessful fair booth as well as comic books and a number of other prizes that were donated by Big Lots, some prizes worth more than others. Bagging up the prizes was extremely time consuming, and as everyone else had enough on their plates, I decided that my new assistant manager and I would take on that chore. He was not pleased with this, feeling that fair managers were above doing such mundane tasks. I guess he never paid attention when I was cleaning toilets. He had a lot to learn.

Everyone was surprised when the event turned out to be successful, despite dire predictions. We had about a hundred families come to participate, and every kid came away with lots of prizes. It wasn't an event as popular as the demolition derbies, but it was good PR and fun for the kids and families—and that's what fairs are about.

CHAPTER TEN
Multiple Grandmothers and Other Carnival Stories

Fair managers and carnival owners see things from different perspectives. After I had run the fair for a few years, I decided that, if I wanted to understand the problems and the business of our strategic partner, I should work for our carnival for a period of time. So, for several years, I spent two weeks in the fall in North Carolina with our carnival company. It was definitely an adventure. I can't say it was exactly enjoyable, but it was eye opening, and I think it's an experience that would be of great benefit to other fair managers.

First of all, the working hours were killers. I often got to the fairgrounds at 7:30 a.m. and didn't leave until well after midnight. I did a variety of things. I counted tickets. I sold tickets. I took pictures. Mostly, I worked in the office counting money. One year I personally counted a million dollars over a ten-day period, and I was in only one of several offices where money was being counted. Carnivals are big businesses, and the better ones are run by intelligent business people, not the stereotypical "carnie." Oh, how they hate that word.

When you think about a carnival, you think about the rides, the foods, and the barkers who try to entice you to play their games on the midway. That's the carnival we see. What we don't see is how it all happens.

In order to get the rides from place to place, carnivals have become trucking companies. They have numerous trucks, all of which need costly permits from every state on whose roads they travel. They also need a fleet of certified drivers. They have mechanics who maintain the trucks, who put the rides together and later take them apart, and who make certain that the rides are assembled properly. No business is complete without people well-versed in marketing, business methods, and accounting. Each location the carnival plays is unique in its design, its availability to water and electricity, and its fire and labor laws. No matter what city they play, carnivals must meet the challenges and be ready to open within a day or two of arrival. That involves a lot of planning and groundwork, which is contrary to the opinion that carnivals are "fly-by-night" operations. Like any other big business, carnival owners have millions of dollars invested in rides and equipment as well as in their reputations; they can't afford to be slip-shod.

But carnival people are definitely unique. They spend the majority of each year traveling. They don't leave their families behind; they take them along. As a result, carnival people are the most family-oriented group I have ever met. They spend 365 days a year with their families, working side-by-side with them in the business, whether it's a food concession, a game trailer, an independently owned ride, or in a position with the administrative staff. Many carnivals have their own school trailers and paid teachers who travel with them. At least in the Northeast, the kids go to school all summer when the carnivals are busy, and they have off between December and February when their families are "home." The kids learn, not only from their teachers, but also from field trips in every location the carnival plays. The kids are happy, well-educated, and surrounded by extended family every day. Not a bad childhood.

I learned that there are two types of carnival workers: the regulars who travel with the carnival all year, and the "green help"— inexperienced people who sign on for one or for a few locations. These are very different groups of people. The regulars usually have their families with them and tend to be reliable. The "green help" may or may not show up on any given day, and the excuses are myriad. They seem to have multiple grandmothers who get sick on a regular basis with illnesses ranging from malaria to leprosy. Because it is so difficult for the carnivals to find employees willing to work long hours and travel all the time, they also rely on immigrant help via the H2-B visa work program. When I was working for them, they had a number of employees from Russia.

The first thing I was asked to do as a carnival worker was to take pictures of the "green help" for name badges. I was handed a digital camera and left on my own. Digital cameras were fairly new at that time, and I had never used one before. I thought I was doing okay until we tried to incorporate the pictures I took onto the ID cards. That's when I discovered that I had been somehow using a negative setting so that everyone had blue faces. It looked like the green help was actually blue help. They asked someone else to re-take the pictures.

Counting money sounds easy, but it turned out to be more complex than I thought. The money was collected by "runners" and brought to the office. Cash was taken multiple times a day from various ticket booths, and at the end of the night, the tickets sold had to correlate with the money collected as well as with the remaining tickets on the rolls we had distributed and documented during the day. There were several different prices of tickets, so keeping everything straight when you have worked for two weeks with little sleep sometimes proved difficult. There were many nights when we didn't leave the fairgrounds until nearly 1 a.m. while we tried to find a mistake. I got better at it as the years went on, but that first year was a lot harder than I imagined it would be.

When you count that volume of money, it ceases to have any magic. The bills become simply pieces of paper with faces on them that you try to match with other pieces of paper with the same faces on them. Even after all the money I handled, I still couldn't tell you whose face is on what bill.

I always liked it when I was sent out as a "runner." At a state fair, the midway is very big, so I usually had to walk quite a distance with a large sum of money before I got back to the office. I was told to be discrete, so I typically shoved the bag of money under my sweatshirt. I'm not sure how discrete that was. I looked like I had a lumpy pregnancy.

At the Monroe County Fair, we always had to deal with summer heat. The North Carolina State Fair is held in October, and the temperature is unpredictable. One year, North Carolina was in the middle of a cold snap. It was about forty degrees with a cold drizzle, and the wind was blowing at a pretty good clip. Instead of the coolest clothing I could find for fair week, I was dressed in layers: long underwear, long-sleeved shirt, sweatshirt, windbreaker, and a winter jacket that I borrowed from Corky that was three sizes too big for me. I huddled into it like a turtle. Nevertheless, there were tons of people on the rides and long lines at the food stands, despite the fact that cotton candy turned to glue before it got it into someone's mouth. Their philosophy was that fairs only come once a year, and if you wait for perfect weather to enjoy them, you will miss out entirely. I wished people in Monroe County had felt that way.

The biggest challenge of working in the office was boredom. Activity happened in spurts, with long intervals between them. I was often alone in the office, so I read. I read ten books that first year, which sounds like a book-lover's dream, but the trailer tilted to one side, had fluorescent lighting, and the only chair in the place was a straight-backed wooden one. Besides being exhausted, I basically ended my carnival stint with eye strain and a crick in my neck.

Food was also a challenge. At the North Carolina State Fair, food came in two varieties: deep fried or with country ham and biscuits. Country ham is like salty shoe leather, and putting it on a biscuit doesn't make it any more palatable. The fried foods were very diverse and tasty: fried apples, fried vegetables, fried apple pie, fried candy bars, fried Twinkies, fried peanut butter and jelly sandwiches—you name it, and I guarantee that somebody at the fairgrounds had a fried version of it. One day towards the end of the fair, a number of us were lamenting our fair food diet, certain we could feel our arteries hardening. One of my office mates brought bologna, bread, and mustard from his trailer. It might not have been particularly nutritious, but at least it wasn't fried. I thought I'd never tasted anything as good.

Corky leant me a brand new pickup truck so I could drive from my hotel to the fairgrounds. I had never driven anything that big before, and I was a nervous wreck, especially when I had to park it. I remember one year in particular. There had been a hurricane just a few days before the fair, so the fairgrounds were muddy and rutted. Shortly after the fair opened, another hurricane came through. Officials decided not to open the fair that day, except nobody remembered to call me at the hotel to tell me. I drove to the fairgrounds, braving torrential rain and wind, finally squeezed the truck into a relatively dry spot, and arrived at the carnival office drenched and somewhat the worse for wear, only to find that the fair was closed. I returned to the truck and reversed the procedure. But getting from the truck back to my hotel room proved to be more of a challenge. By that time, the wind had really picked up, and I was literally hanging on to light poles to keep from being blown over. Moreover, the hotel expected to lose power, and water needed to be boiled, so I was provided with bottled water for drinking, and a flashlight. It was an interesting experience. The next day dawned bright and sunny, and the show went on.

Our fair booked the same midway for a number of years, and I considered the carnival people to be friends. But despite the fact that I knew them well and even worked for them, I always felt like an outsider. It was a close-knit group and, at least at that time, a male-centric one. I could help out, but I could never really be one of them. Still, I always found them willing to assist with any problems our fair faced, and they were invested in seeing our fair succeed. The fair's success was the carnival's success.

But that's not to say that there weren't issues. Even knowing what the carnival's position would be on a particular matter, I sometimes had to put our fair's interests first. And when that happened, the carnival was quick to protest.

Layout was always a challenge. Where I wanted the carnival to be was not always where the carnival wanted to be. Food concessionaires predictably insisted on being front and center. So did my independent food vendors. Little wars ensued. We would set up a lemonade stand, and the carnival would place a lemonade stand directly across from it and charge less for the drinks. Our concessionaires would then complain to our concessions manager who would try to find an amicable solution to the problem, usually unsuccessfully. (Being a fair's concessions manager is a thankless job. By the third day of the fair, whenever the concessions manager was needed somewhere on the fairgrounds, he typically went around the outside of the fair instead of through it in order to avoid being confronted by unhappy vendors.)

Then there was the Great Soda War. Fairs need sponsorships in order to survive. Some of the best sponsors are soft drink distributors. Unfortunately, these sponsorships always come with strings. One of the most hated of stipulations was requiring vendors to serve twelve-ounce bottles of soda instead of using post mix (syrup that is mixed with carbonated water.) Post mix has a much higher profit margin than bottles and is much easier to store. The carnival vendors rebelled. A very irate carnival co-owner appeared in my office, threatening to end the contract with the fair if we continued with this policy. I was between a rock and a hard place. I needed the money, but I also needed the carnival. Eventually, we decided that good will trumped profit, so we abandoned the soda sponsorship and let vendors sell whatever product they liked. The carnival was happy, the vendors were happy, and the public was happy because they had a choice of beverages. I was the only one who wasn't happy since I had lost that particular battle with the bottom line.

Our carnival company usually bought one or two new rides a year, and the spectacular rides cost upwards of a million dollars each. They were things of beauty as well as marvels of physics. I loved to see the carnival at night when all the ride lights were twinkling and pulsing. I don't think a lot of people stop to look at the artistry of the carnival rides, but once I took the time to notice, I found that the nighttime carnival was magical. But as much as I loved *looking* at the rides, I never actually *rode* the rides. Corky even offered to go on The Claw with me, but no friendship (or money) in the world could entice me to hang upside down while forty feet in the air. In truth, I couldn't even watch while my grandchildren were on the rides.

My grandchildren loved to go to "Grandma's fair." They would come every day, and I would give them all-day ride wristbands. They would go on the rides over and over. At the end of the day, they would refuse to take off their wristbands, so by the time fair week was over, they had a colorful collection of wristbands that went from their wrists to their elbows. But even though I knew in my mind that the rides were safe, my heart just wouldn't buy it, and I was always nervous when my grandkids were riding.

According to the carnival people I talked with, carnival rides from reputable carnival companies are actually safer than stationary rides at amusement parks. For one thing, carnival rides are dismantled every week, so the mechanics can see if a part is worn and can replace it immediately. They are then scrutinized daily by carnival personnel. Moreover, carnival rides are meticulously analyzed by independent state inspectors before every fair or festival. That's a lot of inspections. In truth, the incidence of serious accidents on amusement rides as a whole is very low, especially when calculated against the number of times a ride operates in any given year. The Outdoor Amusement Business Association prides itself on maintaining high standards for carnivals and amusement parks and says that "amusement rides constitute one of the safest forms of recreation available to the public."[5] Of course, like anything else that has a lot of mechanical, moving parts, failures can happen. That's why I wanted a carnival that I felt did the best job of maintaining its rides and training its personnel.

By this time, you've probably figured out that I am an obsessive worrier. My philosophy is that as long as I'm worried about something, I have some control over what happens. It's the things I don't worry about that can bite me. So I worried about my grandkids on the rides, and in the barns, and in the grandstand, and pretty much everywhere else. And when they went home, I worried about all the other things that were out of my control.

CHAPTER ELEVEN

Superintendents:
Wonders of the Fair World

Fairs are like giant jigsaw puzzles. There are many different parts, all of which need to come together flawlessly to create the whole picture. There is the carnival piece, the food piece, the commercial piece, the grandstand piece, and the entertainment piece. And then there are all the different departments that make up the competitive piece of the fair: flowers, home arts, livestock, photography, foods, woodworking, and fine arts. Each of these departments has a superintendent whose job it is to find competitors, secure show judges, run the shows, design the exhibits, arrange demonstrations, and staff the exhibits during the duration of the fair.

Finding people willing to donate so much of their time is never an easy task. It isn't a job that just encompasses fair week. It's a year-long commitment that is often thankless. In other words, a superintendent must have a combination of insanity and masochism, along with a love for the fair, or he must have a connection to some member of the fair staff or board who has *lied* to him about what the job is. Once you have found the perfect person for the task, the goal is to never let that person go. That is why many fair superintendents at many fairs are in their eighties and have been running their departments for forty years.

Not all fair superintendents are great, and I had to fire a few. That happened in our Home Arts Department, and as we got close to fair time, I was getting desperate to find someone to fill that vacancy. One of my board members suggested a woman he had met through another board, and Goldee showed up in my office.

I didn't know what to make of Goldee. She was so different from me. I usually dressed in conservative pantsuits or pants and blazers.

That day, Goldee was dressed in a mid-length, loose shift. She wore several necklaces that didn't match the numerous earrings that decorated her ears, each ear sporting a different assortment, along with multiple bracelets on each wrist. She was an artist—eclectic and creative—whereas I was methodical and businesslike. I wondered if we would ever be able to work together.

Over the years, Goldee and I spent a lot of time in each other's company, planning the Home Arts Department, waiting for exhibitors to show up, helping the judges on judging day, and hanging the thousands of community service projects that came in before the fair. Of all the superintendents, I probably spent the most time with Goldee, and as we worked, we talked about family, and problems, and dreams. I found that we weren't so different after all, and we became good friends.

One of the things Goldee and I did on a fairly regular basis was raid junk piles. We were always on the lookout for things we could use as display materials in the Home Arts Department. Someone's discarded porch steps were ideal for showcasing small objects that could be tiered. Cupboards without doors also made interesting exhibit pieces. Over the years, we amassed quite a number of what Goldee called our "primo junk." My maintenance staff would shudder when I told them to pick up stuff from a curb someplace. They knew they would not only have to transport it, but also have to fix it, paint it, and then find a place to store it.

There was a large building in downtown Rochester that was the home of Sibley's, one of the most prominent department stores in the area. The building had large, first floor display windows that fronted on Main Street. Every Christmas, the decorators at Sibley's would design elaborate tableaus for those windows that people would flock to see. When Sibley's closed in 1990, the lower floors of the building remained largely vacant for a number of years, but the building manager made the show windows available to nonprofits. Goldee found out about this, and every year, she arranged for us to have a window for the month before the fair. We would paw through our "primo junk," truck it all downtown, and decorate the window in the fair's theme for that year. I say that "we" decorated the window. In reality, Goldee artistically designed the tableau, and I put stuff wherever she told me. It was a great way for us to advertise for the fair, and it cost us practically nothing, which was always a plus.

Goldee and her husband customarily spent the winter months in California, visiting with her step-daughters, so I usually didn't see her from late autumn to April. One spring, she came to the fairgrounds to check in. She had lost a great deal of weight over the winter, and I was very concerned. She looked gaunt. Shortly thereafter, she was diagnosed with stage four ovarian cancer, and a year and a half later, she was dead.

Goldee loved the fair, and as sick as she was, she took the time to come to the fair to see the Home Arts Department that first summer, leaning heavily on her sister as she viewed the exhibits. After her death, the Home Arts Committee decided that the Best of Show prize in that department would bear Goldee's name. I still miss her. She was unique, a good person, and a good friend.

When Goldee got sick, I asked Judy if she could pitch in as superintendent, and because Judy is such a lovely person, she agreed. I knew Judy from when I worked for 4-H at Cornell Cooperative Extension. She was an extension agent and had recently retired. I must admit that I downplayed the time commitment involved, but Judy stuck with me for many years. We are still friends, and I think she has forgiven me for misleading her.

The Flower Department was another huge undertaking. We had a relatively new board member who, although not an avid gardener, had entered garlic in the fair's flower show competition. By some sleight of tongue, I convinced Sal that he should become the Flower Superintendent. He had been a manager at Xerox before he retired, and he was used to running a tight ship. Fairs tend to be more like leaky canoes than tight ships, so both the fair staff and Sal had to make adjustments. But what a job he did! He brought in garden clubs and celebrity judges and worked with the Hosta Society for a one-day hosta show. The Flower Department was never better. He stayed with us for a number of years and left the department in good hands when he finally retired to tend his garlic.

Sal and Theresa Madonna, Flower Show Superintendents

Supervising the livestock barn was always a challenge. Not only were there several different departments involved in the overall area (dairy cattle, beef cattle, goats, sheep, rabbits, cavies, pigeons, and poultry), but there was the matter of supervising all the kids who stayed in the barn for the duration of the fair. Needless to say, those superintendents had a high turnover rate. Of them all, my favorite was someone we'll call Mrs. M. She was feisty and took no guff from anyone. Exhibitors can be mean and petty, especially when confined in a smelly barn for a week with a bunch of animals that needed to be fed, brushed, and kept clean. (And that was just the kids.) There were cows and goats to milk, stalls to clean, milk to dispose of, and the ever-present fly population that needed to be kept under control for the health (physical and mental) of the exhibitors. Mrs. M. dealt with them all, and I loved her for dealing with them so that I didn't have to. She took care of runaway rabbits, pigeons that literally flew the coop and flitted around the exhibit hall, sheep that keeled over and died, and cows that gave birth on site.

Every year, we had an amateur talent show at the fair. It was the job of our summer intern to find celebrity judges for this show. A prime place to start was at local radio and TV stations that usually had on-air personalities who were willing to participate in community events. One day my intern, who happened to be my son, Michael, told me that, "Some guy, whose last name I can't pronounce or spell, who is a news anchor, is interested in coming to the fair and doing a lot of stuff." Plus, he wanted to bring his friend, who was a former Miss New York State, and who was now the director of the Mrs. New York America Pageant, with him. I told Michael not to let the guy get away, and a wonderful new partnership was born with Gary (whose last name, incidentally, is Tschaepe pronounced "Chaffie") and Joanne Cercone.

Gary was a big man—not fat, just very, very tall. He had a booming laugh, an engaging personality, and he dominated every room he entered. Joanne was barely five feet tall and a hundred pounds, but she was a force to be reckoned with. She knew what she wanted, wasn't afraid to ask for it, and did a bang-up job with everything she undertook. Although not a couple, they were great friends, and they soon became great friends of the fair as well. Not only did they judge our talent shows, but Gary also acted as its Master of Ceremonies. Eventually, Joanne became the talent show superintendent, bringing professionalism to the contest, and soon, we had enough acts to expand the show to three days. She also brought current and former Mrs. New York Americas to the fair as judges and to participate in promotional parades. These women became part of our fair family along with Gary and Joanne.

Because they were so willing and seemed to enjoy their involvement with the fair, I used them shamelessly. Both were talented singers, so I always asked them to perform at the fair or at promotional events, and I don't think they ever refused me. They also were instrumental in getting The Fair Kids launched. Gary eventually moved to Florida, and I lost track of him, but Joanne and I are still good friends, and she is as an honorary aunt to two of my grandchildren.

We had horse shows almost every day of the fair, and since horse people are notoriously particular, this was one of the more intense volunteer positions as well as one that had a lot of turnover.

One of our horse superintendents was Jay. She was a little bit of a woman with a huge personality, and she did wonders with a horse arena that was really not up to a horseman's standards. Her love of horses and her ability to deal with different personalities made her an invaluable volunteer, but what I most remember about her was her relationship with the two-way radio we gave her. She had no faith in it. Whenever she needed someone, she would yell into it, "Hello? Is anyone out there?" When we answered her, she always gave an audible sigh of relief.

Kirstie came after Jay, and she was a wonder. She not only kept everyone happy, but she managed to find prizes, decorations, and help (whom she called "her minions") at almost no cost to the fair. She was a Class A scrounger, a skill she had finely honed. If given enough time, she could find almost anything at no cost. With our strangled budget, this was a highly prized skill.

Jay and Kirstie were patient and knowledgeable with both the horses and their riders, and they created an amazing agricultural experience for our urban fairgoers as they managed events that included formal English riding as well as freewheeling barrel racing. Amid the clamor of the fair, audiences found it peaceful to view the grazing horses. Then they watched with excitement as riders soared over higher and still higher jumps inside the stark white fences of the show ring. The draft horse show—with the Percherons, the Belgians, and the Clydesdales—was always a fair favorite. Majestic and awe-inspiring, the huge horses trotted around the arena with their heads held high. Their harnesses jingled with silver bells, and the clomping of their enormous feet could be heard even above the raucous sounds of the fair. The superintendents superbly managed these diverse horse shows—events that hearkened back to America's heritage.

I am eternally grateful to all our superintendents, those named and those who shall remain anonymous. Some came back year after year, and some came only for a season, but I couldn't have run the fair without them. Although they received a small stipend, it was no more than a token considering the amount of work we required of them as well as the tremendous time commitment. They were vital extensions of our small fair staff, and they made it possible for us to put on a quality event.

CHAPTER TWELVE

The Others

When you have hundreds of volunteers, there are always some who don't work out well. I hate confrontation, so I tended to try to accommodate everyone's idiosyncrasies. But at fair time, my tolerance level went way down as did my ability to be accommodating.

A man we'll call Mr. R. was superintendent of the rabbit barn. He was one of those people who had held the post since before time began. He had his way of doing things. That's the way they had always been done and that's the way they were always going to be done. End of discussion. Enter a new fair manager, and fur was sure to fly. Times had changed. I wanted health checks for rabbits before they were allowed into the fair. I wanted there to be water in the rabbits' cages at all times, no matter how often the animals dumped their water bowls. I wanted the cages cleaned more than once in the week. I insisted. He resisted. Finally, it came down to my way or the highway. He chose the highway. One of my former 4-H kids, now an adult, took over as superintendent. She had been a teen when I became leader of the 4-H rabbit club, and she was the one who taught me the most about rabbits. She did a fine job as superintendent and worked with me for many years, as did other members of local rabbit clubs.

I inherited someone who we'll refer to as Mrs. V. when I became fair manager. An elderly, heavy-set woman with steel-gray hair, she was the fair's show secretary. It was her job to see that all of the exhibits (animals, flowers, baked goods, home arts, etc.) were entered in the correct classes and that entry fees were paid. Following the shows, she needed to record the winners and prepare prize money checks. Like Mr. R., Mrs. V. had been doing the job since time immemorial, and she didn't want any interference. I don't think she liked people very much, so she wasn't exactly a pleasant person with whom to deal. She had a cane, and whenever she was unhappy about something, she would bang her cane on the floor to emphasize her displeasure. Exhibitors tried to avoid her. So did I.

Mrs. V. had an office in the Dome that had an individual air conditioner. There was a problem with one of the shows, and I needed to straighten out the books. I went into her office and spent two hours figuring out the problem. It was about ninety degrees outside, and by the time I was done sorting things out, I was drenched with sweat. I couldn't figure out why the air conditioner wasn't cooling the room. That's when I discovered that instead of the air setting, Mrs. V. had turned the dial to heat. I prefer to think it was unintentional on her part, not done just to torture me, but who knows?

Mrs. V. had a parking spot that she had used for all the eons she had been show secretary. The problem was that we had changed the fair layout, and parking there was not possible. She insisted that she be allowed to use that spot, and no amount of explaining why she couldn't, satisfied her. I finally told her that she could park in my parking space, the closest she was going to get, and that I would personally pick her up in a golf cart and bring her to her office. At the end of the day, I would bring her back to her car. She refused and said that if she couldn't park in her usual location, she was leaving and wasn't coming back. As I mentioned, it was not wise to push me too far during fair week. I snapped.

"Fine. Don't," I said, and I slammed the door behind me as I left her office. And she didn't. We managed.

The Grange president was another veteran volunteer with whom I had parking issues. He insisted on parking his van as close to the Grange's food booth as he could, which was usually in the middle of the road. I had an ongoing argument with him about moving his van—every single day.

George, however, was a wonderful surprise. He stopped by the office one day and asked if I could provide him with a list of carnival companies because he was looking for a midway for a church festival. As he was pleasant and personable, I got to chatting with him and learned that he had been the executive director of the Fair Association when the Dome was built and during the fair's heyday in the 1970s. As we talked, I could tell he hadn't lost his enthusiasm for the fair. He assured me that once "fair fever" bit you, you would never shake it off. It didn't take much to convince him to get involved with the fair once again, and before long, he was on our board of directors and chair of the fair committee. He was a wonderful asset and resource, and I know he enjoyed his re-involvement with us. He became the fair's official photographer and took thousands of pictures. The only problem with his pictures was that he usually took them before we opened, so it was difficult to use them for publicity purposes without having the fair look like a vast wasteland. But George was my friend and mentor, and I was never sorry that I convinced him to hook up with us again.

Concessionaires were always a mixed bag. Some were so nice and helpful and grateful to be part of the fair. Others were a trial. Mr. L. was both. He was a large man who had a prime location on a busy corner of the fairgrounds, so he had no reason to be unhappy. But he liked to sit on that corner and pontificate. I could never walk by without him telling me about all the things I was doing wrong. Then he would turn around and give me a free drink and book his space for the following year. It's hard to decide whether he was a blessing or a curse.

Mr. W. was an agitator. Whenever traffic was slow, he would rile up the other concessionaires and complain or demand a refund of his space rental. He was not someone that we enjoyed having on our midway. Mr. W. sold grilled chicken. Chicken is a highly perishable food, and the storage of raw chicken is stringently regulated by the Health Department. One day, our concessions manager was walking by and noticed that Mr. W. was storing his uncooked chicken in the trunk of his car. Mr. W. was asked to leave, and the fair went a lot smoother.

Then there were the concessionaires who had other gigs booked for the weekends. They would come to our fair for a few days and then disappear in the middle of the night on Thursday to go to more lucrative locations. That really wasn't very wise. Fair managers talk to each other.

The people in the front office were crucial parts of the fair. They set the tone with exhibitors or the public who came looking for advice, or to complain, or because they had a lost child. Over my twenty years at the fair, I had fourteen different secretaries. Some lasted only a short time and some were with me for many years. It was a hard position to fill because I needed someone with expertise in technology, to compensate for my lack of same, as well as someone who could get along with all sorts of people and make the office a pleasant place. Some of the women who staffed that desk were great and others cast a pall over the office. I will mention a few of them.

Number Four was a beautiful young girl with dark hair and eyes, creamy skin, and a killer figure. She was so beautiful that many of the male show promoters, who seldom interacted with the office staff, suddenly found reasons to stop by the office. She only worked for me for a few months, much to the disappointment of most of the males who did business with us.

My daughter replaced Number Four. She had just graduated from college and needed a job; I needed a secretary. It was a match made in heaven, at least from my point of view. To hear her tell it, it was a match made in purgatory. She said that the people in the town complained about everything, and that most of her days were spent fielding those complaints. She did a great job for me, though. In fact, of my fourteen secretaries, she was the only one who actually made the morning coffee and straightened my office. She left me when she got married and moved to Albany.

Number Six was someone we loved to have in the office. Blond and blue eyed, she had a sunny personality to match her looks. She kept us all happy. If anything bothered her, she would try to find "her happy place," and we would all go there with her. She kept us grounded and laughing during some very stressful times. I was sad when she left to take a better paying job, but she always came back to help at the fair.

Number Nine was a recent college graduate, but she apparently never took Work Ethics 101 because she didn't seem to understand that "work" actually meant that you had to do something. She spent most of her time on the phone talking with friends, including a day-long conversation about a dinner party she was planning. She lasted three weeks.

As for the others, one hated answering the phone and instituted what we called "the pop and drop." She would engage a call and immediately end it. Another would have periodic crying jags and lock herself in the bathroom. Still another took her role as gatekeeper so seriously that she scared everybody—including me. One had the face of an angel and the mouth of a trucker, and there was one the staff disliked, and one who disliked the staff. None of these secretaries lasted long.

Number Thirteen, my (almost) final secretary, stayed with me on and off for many years. When I think about my secretary, she is the one that immediately comes to mind. She had health issues, so she was sometimes gone for several months at a time, during which we would either get a substitute (Number Fourteen, who was wonderful but who lacked computer skills) or my staff and I would take turns at the reception desk. When Number Thirteen was healthy, she was great. She was a big woman with an infectious smile and a butch haircut "because it's easier." She was good with people, a whiz on the computer, and could multi-task better than anyone I knew. She could handle having five people waiting to talk to her, the two-way radio blaring, and four telephone lines ringing, without batting an eye. But she hated the fair's Youth Day with a passion and claimed that she finally understood why some animals eat their young. We usually steered clear of her on that day.

She also had coulrophobia—a fear of clowns. We used clowns sparingly at the fair because kids tended to be afraid of them too, but one year we booked Ronald McDonald for Youth Day. We warned my secretary in advance that he was going to be at the fair, and his handler snuck him into my office when my secretary was out to lunch. However, no one had thought to inform me that the clown was in my office, and it scared the hell out of me when I wandered in for a break and was confronted with a white-faced, red-nosed, fully grown clown who was sitting at my conference table staring at me. I think I now have coulrophobia, too.

I had the best staff anyone could imagine. There were ten of us: a part-time bookkeeper, an events manager, a marketing and sales director, a secretary-receptionist, a maintenance supervisor, and four general maintenance workers. Each one of them had idiosyncrasies, but they all had a love for the fair, and I knew I could always count on them. We supplemented our small staff with additional people during the fair, but we were still only a small group when you consider the monumental job we had to do. And in reality, the staff performed miracles. With a limited budget, we all worked long hours and did things that, in retrospect, were impossible. For example, on Youth Day, we usually had about 3,500 kids that came to the fair between 10 a.m. and 4 p.m. The fair opened to the public at 4 p.m. After the kids left, the fairgrounds were a shambles. Upended chairs, tables laden with half-eaten food, discarded cups, bottles, juice boxes, sneakers, stray pieces of clothing, overflowing garbage cans—you name it—were visible in the wake of the kids. Yet by 4:15, the grounds were spotless and ready for our night-time guests.

My philosophy was that I never asked staff to do anything I was not willing to do myself (except for things that involved heights . . . and vomit.) That included cleaning bathrooms when no one else was available, or picking up trash. I knew my staff was loyal to me and I was loyal to them. I felt that my job as manager was to get the best out of them and to ignore their quirks. As a result, we had an unbelievable staff that I very much valued. Unfortunately, some members of my board only focused on the quirks and never appreciated their spectacular efforts. I found that very disheartening.

Throughout the years, I had some interesting characters on my board. Two of them bear mentioning.

My favorite of all was someone we'll call Mr. H. Mr. H. was the personification of the word "gentleman." His age was eighty-something, and he always dressed in his best coat and tie. A colorful vest invariably peaked out from under his coat, and a jaunty beret perched on his head of abundant, snow-white hair. I never saw him without a pipe in his mouth, and I could always tell when Mr. H. was around by the fragrance of the tobacco he smoked. He was our sound technician as well as being on the board, so I would see him frequently as he set up microphones and speakers for our various shows.

Mr. H. loved music and he loved to dance. His wife had died long before I met him, and I suspect he was pretty lonely after her death, but he seemed to have found a family among our fair staff. He spent a good deal of his time just "poking about" or having a cup of coffee with "the boys" in our break room. One day, I happened upon him as he was setting up speakers in Minett Hall. Thinking he was alone in the building, he was listening to music with the speakers turned up to a deafening volume while he danced a beautiful waltz with an invisible partner. I snuck away before he saw me, leaving him to his daydream.

Mr. H. was also a pack rat. He had commandeered several rooms as well as a building on the fairgrounds where he stored his sound equipment, and each room was crammed with paraphernalia that had long since stopped working. He sometimes made half-hearted attempts to organize, but since he couldn't bear to part with anything, the debris just continued to gather.

I eventually learned that Mr. H.'s hoarding was not limited to the fairgrounds. One cold night in January, I was working late at my desk when Mr. H. popped into my office. He said he had misplaced his car keys and asked if I could drive him home. He had become quite forgetful as the years went on, and his eyesight was also failing, so I offered to help him look for his keys. After unsuccessfully searching for quite some time, I agreed to take him home. As we were driving, I asked if he had a key to his house. He responded that the house key was on the same ring as his car key, but he said that a friend had promised to stop by to open the door for him. He had no idea what time that might actually occur.

It was already eleven o'clock at night, and the temperature had dropped to below zero. I told Mr. H. that I couldn't just leave him outside with only the possibility that his friend would eventually drop by. He thought he had a house key hidden in the garage, and after several attempts to pull up the door, he finally succeeded in gaining entrance to the garage.

The garage was filled, wall-to-wall, with stuff. He wiggled his way between boxes and miscellaneous equipment of an indeterminate nature, and disappeared for several minutes. When he returned, he said that he had been unsuccessful in locating a key. However, he indicated that there was a partially opened bathroom window in the front of the house, and he decided that he could climb in that window to get inside. He pulled over a bench and, with wobbling legs, proceeded to pull himself up onto it. Putting aside my fear of heights, I told him to get down and to let me do the gymnastics of crawling through the window, since I was at least twenty-five years younger than he was. But in true gentlemanly fashion, he insisted that he be the one to do it. Before I could protest, he dove, head first, into the bathroom. All I heard was a thump and then the sound of things falling. My heart in my mouth, I jumped onto the bench and peered in the open window. Mr. H. had landed between the toilet and the sink, and he was wedged in by a multitude of boxes that had been crammed into the room. I managed to lean far enough into the window so that he could grab my arm, and, with some difficulty, I pulled him into a standing position. He calmly thanked me, pushed aside the numerous boxes, walked to the front door, and opened it from the inside. Although he had a gash on his head that he didn't seem to notice, he seemed none the worse for wear. I, on the other hand, was a wreck.

Another one of my favorite characters was Mr. X. In truth, he could best be described as a curmudgeon. At board or committee meetings, he always asked the tough questions that had to be asked but that nobody wanted to answer. Although he was frequently a pain in the ass, I appreciated the fact that he really cared about the Fair Association and wasn't averse to ruffling feathers on its behalf. He could be a wonderful ally or a fierce adversary, and I grudgingly liked him despite his disagreeable disposition. When he died, I believe I was the only board member to attend his wake, and I actually shed a tear for the loss of a man who was truly the conscience of the board.

CHAPTER THIRTEEN
Fairus

The Fair Committee decided that we needed a mascot, so we searched through catalogs and eventually settled on a purple cow. At least that's what we thought it was. Other people thought it was a pig, or a bull, or a "what the heck is that?" Anyway, it was a light purple, plush animal of some sort. It had a smashed-in nose, hence the pig reference, and a yellow hat that sprouted horns. Its smiling face was actually at chest level for the person wearing it, which was kind of disconcerting if you were female. The line of sight for the unlucky person inside the suit was through the hat. The costume, which included mittens and booties, covered the wearer from head to toe. Needless to say, it was hot as hell wearing it in the middle of the July heat. Eventually, we got an ice vest that resulted in the wearer freezing his chest while the rest of him sweated like a pig—or a cow.

We named the mascot "Fairus" meaning "fair us." Everyone wanted to be Fairus—once. That was usually enough because Fairus was very difficult to handle. Not only was it a hot costume to wear, but it was also difficult to see where you were going when wearing it. You could only see directly in front of you and had no peripheral vision. Venturing forth without a handler was disastrous.

One evening, when no one else was available, I agreed to don the costume for a Rochester Redwings mascot night. Upon Fairus' appearance, one of two things was likely to happen: a small child would scream and run toward Fairus for a hug, nearly knocking her (him?) over, or a small child would scream in terror and run in the other direction. Sometimes, those two things happened simultaneously. But it wasn't the toddlers who were the problems. It was the seven-to-nine-year-olds who would come up behind Fairus and pull its tail or jump on its back. I was besieged by such boys as I tried to negotiate the stairs at the baseball stadium. I finally turned around and told them that I was the principal at their school, and if they didn't cut it out, they were going to be in big trouble. I never saw them again, but I bet they were confused when school started in the fall.

We usually convinced my son, Michael, to be Fairus, until he got too tall to wear the costume. But before that happened, we sent him to many mascot events so he could represent the fair. One such event was a Rochester Amerks hockey game. During intermission, mascots that represented different organizations and businesses were called onto the ice for a broom-hockey match. Michael was at a decided disadvantage in such a game because his sight was limited, and he couldn't move very fast with the costume's short legs and cumbersome, plush body. Nevertheless he gave it a try, and actually succeeding in scoring a goal while simultaneously wiping out the little, pig-tailed Wendy mascot, whom he couldn't see. They both fell to the ice, but Fairus couldn't get up. The crowd loved it—Wendy not so much.

We also sent Fairus to parades, building floats on which the mascot could ride. We tried to make every parade we possibly could. It was cheap advertising for the fair and got us in front of a lot of people very quickly.

Our first floats were quite limited. We borrowed a board member's small trailer, the kind used by commercial landscapers to haul riding mowers. We decorated it with flowers and signs, and Fairus rode in the back and threw candy to the on-lookers. The trailer was small enough to be pulled by the fair's pickup truck or, in a pinch, by my station wagon. I usually had our summer intern or a member of the maintenance staff pull the trailer—except once. No one but me was available to drive in the Harbor Festival parade. With great reluctance, I resigned myself to doing it. The problem was that I couldn't back up with a trailer hitched to my car. I planned the route and was confident that I could drive forward the whole time and not have to contend with backing up. That worked until the police closed the roads, forcing all the floats to park until the parade was over.

I pulled into a parking space and waited until all the other floats had departed. And then I tried to back up. And then I tried to back up. And then I tried to back up. Finally, I got out of my station wagon, unhitched the trailer, manually turned it around and then backed my car up to the trailer and reconnected the hitch. That was my first and last time pulling a trailer.

There is a major festival in Rochester called the Lilac Festival that is held annually in the middle of May. It prides itself on being very prestigious, and when I was running the county fair, the Lilac Festival organizers looked down their noses at us (or maybe it was just my paranoia.) To kick off the festival, there was a Lilac Parade, and we decided that we wanted to be part of it. I requested a participation application, and we waited and waited. I never heard from the organizers. I finally called, and asked why we had never received an application. I could almost feel the disdain over the phone. We eventually got the application and the approval to have a float in the parade, but I knew we had to up our game.

We found a local farmer who was willing to donate a flatbed wagon to us and who would let us keep it for a few weeks while we decorated it and used it in both the Lilac Parade and in the Town of Henrietta's Memorial Day Parade that was the following week. We placed our gazebo on the flatbed and decorated the whole float with flowers and wooden cut-outs of various livestock. Our mascot would stand in the middle of the gazebo and wave to the crowds.

At the last minute, we learned that with the gazebo atop the flatbed, the float was too high to fit under the power lines along the parade route, so we had to tear off the roof. The float actually looked pretty cool and very modern minus the gazebo's roof, and we finished with a first place ribbon. Thereafter, we automatically received a yearly invitation to participate in the parade.

Pulling a float that large required a certain class of driver's license. One of my board members, Mr. T., who was an elderly farmer, had such a license and agreed to drive the truck for the Henrietta parade. At the end of the parade route, we had to go around a very long block in order to get back to the fairgrounds. I don't know if Mr. T. forgot he was pulling a trailer with people on it or if he always drove like a bat out of hell, but the people on the float were hanging on for dear life, ducking under overhanging tree branches, and fending off flowers that were blowing off the float at an alarming rate. When the truck came to a stop, the people were actually hugging each other and crying in relief.

Sometimes we only decorated my car, and people, like the Fair Kids, walked behind it. It's not easy driving in a parade, and I hated it. You have to be careful that you don't ram into whatever is ahead of you. I always worried (of course) about kids running in front of my car as they tried to get to pieces of candy thrown from other floats. As a result, my hands were usually locked onto the steering wheel with my foot riding the brake pedal for the duration of the parade.

Like fairs, parades are affected by the weather. The Lilac Parade was especially prone to adverse conditions because it was held in early May. Spring in Rochester doesn't come until late May. Since the Lilac Parade was a week or so before that, it was usually still cold and drizzly or outright pouring. If Fairus was difficult to manipulate when dry, he was an impossible, soggy, plushy mess when wet, which happened on more than one occasion.

I had such a limited budget that we were always looking for ways to get the word out about the fair without spending a lot of money. Parades and mascot appearances were some of our best efforts, and we got a lot of mileage out of them.

Our Lilac Festival float in 2007

Diving Horses and Pigs—Oh My!

Over the years, we had many different kinds of entertainment at the fair. We were always trying to find that one thing that would draw in thousands of people. We usually tried to match the entertainment to the fair's theme for that year. One year, our theme was "Under the Big Top" and we hired a three-ring circus. Mostly, people seemed disinterested in that, and the performances had only half-filled seats. Obviously that was not the magic bullet we'd expected.

The year we had the space station exhibit, our theme was "Exploring Frontiers." Our entertainment included a cowgirl who did trick roping and Doc Barth who had an old-time medicine show. The space station didn't draw as we had hoped and neither did the Western acts. But that year, I became acquainted with Doc (Dan) Barth.

Dan is a big man in the John Wayne style of big. His skin is always deeply tanned, and I never saw him without his trademark Stetson. Dan is a storyteller, a ventriloquist, a historian, and a humorist, and his show is part of the living history of the West. Dan could talk for hours about his experiences on the road and about the pageantry of medicine shows, and I never tired of listening to him. He has performed for over forty years, not only at fairs and festivals, but also at the White House, on Broadway, for a TV series called *America on Tour,* and at the 1996 Olympics, among other things. We only booked him at the fair once, but I think I talked to him every year just to catch up on his latest adventures.

Of all the entertainment we had at the fair, it was the racing pigs that consistently drew crowds. The performances only lasted about ten minutes each, but there were a lot of performances throughout the day. It was always standing room only. One year we had the racing and diving pigs, which was really funny. It turns out that pigs love to swim.

Racing pigs at the 2010 fair, photo by Bill Pfeifer

We also had "the Incredible Diving Horse," which was truly . . . incredible. Diving horses were introduced in the 1880s at the Atlantic City Steel Pier, and they became popular attractions at fairs and carnivals until the late 1970s.[6] The movie *Wild Hearts Can't Be Broken* was filmed in 1991 and was about the diving horses and their trainer, Sonora Webster Carter. The entertainer that we had at our fair was probably one of the few remaining people who had a horse that was trained to dive off a forty-foot platform into a pool of water. With today's emphasis on and awareness of animal welfare issues, we probably would not book this show, but at the time, it was well-received—a marvel for fairgoers.

The year after we did the alligator show, we had "The Shark Encounter." This show consisted of a 5,000 gallon tank that contained three nurse sharks that were three-and-a-half-to-seven feet long. The emcee got into the tank with the sharks and spoke to the audience through an underwater microphone. I didn't think that watching the sharks was as much fun as watching the hunky alligator wrestlers, but we endeavored to keep the fair fresh by bringing in something new every year (although I wouldn't have minded seeing the hunky alligator wrestlers again.)

We tried a lot of different bands on our Festival Tent stage, but only three of them had a following that actually drew people to the fair.

Ballbreaker, an AC/DC cover band, was by far our biggest attraction, and the Festival Tent was always full whenever they played. Ed Spock, the lead singer, had worked for me for a number of years, and he was one of my favorite people. I always made it a point to stop by the Festival Tent to listen to his band. It turns out that I like AC/DC, which my staff found hilarious. Who knew?

Another act that always did well for us was Josie Waverly. Josie is a local country singer with a crossover to gospel. She has a gorgeous voice and has opened for a number of big name country stars. The locals loved her and so did we. She was always sweet and accommodating, and she performed for us many times, usually to standing room only audiences,

Ruby Shooz, a 50s-60s party band, still has a large following across Western New York. No matter what time of the day or night they played, they always had people dancing in the aisles. They continue to perform at local festivals and even at some of the casinos around the state.

Our talent shows were always packed because the performers brought their grandmothers, aunts, uncles, friends, and anyone they could coerce into coming to cheer them on. We loved it. Some of the performers were mediocre, but some of them were really talented. I remember one girl in particular. Her name was Ashley Harrington, and she was twelve years old when I first heard her sing. She had an amazingly mature voice, and if you weren't looking at her, you would think she was an adult. Through the years, her voice just got better and better. She often sang one of my favorites, Puccini's "O Mio Babbino Caro" from the opera *Gianni Schicchi*, so when I knew she was performing, I made time to go to the Festival Tent. I'd sit in the back, close my eyes, and let her beautiful voice wash over me. For that little while, I was transported from the clamor of the fair to a peaceful place filled with beautiful music. I always blinked when I opened my eyes, trying to reorient myself to my location.

Larry Moss was just starting out when I first met him in 1992. He had been a street performer in New York City, doing magic tricks and juggling, but he was fairly new to Rochester. In fact, I believe we gave him his first major gig in the area when he performed for us as a court jester doing magic tricks. He got into creating balloon sculptures, and his career really took off. Today he has created balloon sculptures internationally, and in 2015 he was named by the *Washington Post* as "the best balloon artist in the world."

One of my favorite bands was the Towpath Volunteers Fife and Drum Corps. We had them at the fair when our theme was "A Snapshot of America." They were dressed in colonial garb, and between the costumes and the Sousa marches, I always had tears in my eyes when they played. I think fair people tend to be extremely patriotic, and the performances of the Towpath Volunteers pushed all the right patriotic buttons for me.

We had a number of different promoters who did our demolition derbies. I think the best was J.M. Productions. The company did derbies all over the state, including the New York State finals that were held at the State Fair. They even did stunts for major films and had the famous James Bond car that appeared in the movie *The Man with the Golden Gun*. I wasn't a big fan of the original J.M., but I loved his son and daughter-in-law, who eventually took over the business. Whenever they came to the fair, it was like seeing family.

Charlie Belknap was another favorite of mine. From 1990-2005, he was the owner and general manager of the Toyota Hollywood Stunt Show, an attraction that was booked at plus or minus ninety-four events per year. Charlie produced and choreographed the shows during which his drivers sped through fire and jumped over numerous cars. He also coordinated stunts for movies and television shows. Even though we only booked the Toyota Hollywood Stunt Show a couple of times, I always enjoyed talking with Charlie since he played fairs all over the country and had a good understanding of what worked well at them. When he eventually left the stunt show business, he worked in marketing for several carnivals, a perfect fit for skills he learned from his years on the show circuit.

The trade shows at the state and national conventions were great places to find the unusual entertainment that is traditionally presented at fairs—from duck races to Elvis impersonators. They were also great places to catch up with some of the performers we'd used at previous fairs, like Oscar the Robot and his handler, Jack Prather, and Dan Barth. I don't think I ever met a performer I didn't like. They have a hard life traveling from place to place, but they are down-to-earth people and always interesting.

CHAPTER FIFTEEN
Youth Day!
(Can I Take My Vacation Now?)

Youth Days are traditional parts of fairs. Youth groups are given advanced-sale discount tickets and are allowed to come to the fair when it's not open to the public. When I first came to our fair, we had about 500 kids who took advantage of this day. I decided we could do better.

In early February 1993, before summer recreation schedules were set, I arranged appointments with recreation directors in every town in Monroe County, which meant I was covering 657 square land miles that encompassed twenty towns, all in the worst month of the year for winter driving. With map in hand, I had to somehow find my way to twenty town office buildings. I always allowed myself an extra half-hour in case I got lost. (Okay, I added an extra hour because I always got lost, especially if I was going to the western part of the county with which I was unfamiliar. Then, no matter where I was headed, I always seemed to end up on the Hamlin Beach State Parkway, which has almost no exits for turnarounds.) I personally extended invitations to recreation directors to consider the fair as one of their planned field trips. I also visited all four YMCAs (located in four corners of the county) as well as private organizations that advertised summer camps. It was a busy winter but a fruitful one. That summer, we had 2,500 kids for Youth Day.

In addition, we did what we called "Special Time for Special People" where we invited kids with physical and mental disabilities from group homes and programs to come to the fair for free on the day before the fair opened to the public. The carnival agreed to open appropriate rides, and we always served the groups lunch. The Moose Club sponsored the day, and we asked service clubs, like Kiwanis, to cook and serve the hot dog lunches. Additionally, each kid got a goody bag to take back. It was a very successful day and very heartwarming for us, but it became problematic. If it was too hot (and it was usually too hot) or too rainy (ditto), the groups would not come—or if they did come, it was not very enjoyable for them. When it rained, the carnival had to close the rides due to safety concerns, which was very disappointing to the kids. One year, it rained so hard that the kids not only couldn't get on rides, but they also got soaked and ended up eating their cold hot dogs on waterlogged buns.

"Special Times" was labor intensive and time-consuming for the staff at a point when we had neither time nor energy to spare, so after the soggy hot dog bun year, we decided to incorporate that event into our Youth Day. We would no longer serve lunch, but the kids would still have free admission and unlimited ride wristbands. By that time, our "Special Times" kids numbered about 1,000, so this upped our Youth Day to 3,500 attendees.

Youth Day was always scheduled to start at 10 a.m. Invariably, by 8:30 a.m., the first buses began arriving. Since the carnival was geared to open at 10 a.m., this meant the kids had to wait for an hour-and-a-half before they could be admitted, which was a bit of a problem for the hapless counselors who had to corral them. But the buses just kept on coming. Some years, we had twenty or thirty of them, all with drivers trying to find places to park that weren't mud bogs.

Most recreation centers preordered their wristbands and received them in the mail, which really expedited things. But some of them didn't know until the day of the event how many kids were coming, so they bought their wristbands at the gate. Others needed extra wristbands, so we sent most of the office staff to the gate to facilitate these purchases. It was a madhouse with group leaders trying to count heads, keep everyone in line, determine who had a wristband and who didn't, or wait for another leader to come who actually had the wristbands that could be distributed. Groups usually had color-specific t-shirts so that counselors could keep track of who belonged to whom.

That worked well except with the preschoolers who had no clue what was going on and tended to wander off. I felt sorry for the summer interns who were tasked with keeping track of the groups of too-hot-too-excited kids, most of whom couldn't follow directions. When seeing the chaos, I *almost* felt guilty about encouraging recreation directors to send their kids to the fair.

Each group also brought huge coolers that contained lunches and drinks for their participants. It was a trek from the parking lot to the midway, and that first year, we watched the counselors struggling to carry the heavy coolers until they found a place to set up for the day. After that, we enlisted our maintenance staff to transport the coolers via golf cart to wherever the group leaders designated. This worked well and saved the leaders, who were already over-taxed, from heat exhaustion. It was also a good selling point for us because it showed we were responsive to the needs of our customers.

We had lots of tables set up on the grounds: picnic tables, tables in the (not open for business) Beer Tent, tables in the Festival Tent, and white plastic tables and chairs in an open food court area. We thought we had set up enough of them until I walked into my office and found a group eating lunch at my conference table. (That conference table had a life of its own!) I'm not sure which startled me more: the clown or the group of twelve who were devouring pizza. The following year, we set up more tables everywhere: inside the Dome lobby, on the patio that was the entrance to the flower show, and anywhere we could find a bit of shade. All the tables were used and, by the time the kids left, the fairgrounds looked like a hurricane had come through.

With that many kids on the grounds, we spent a lot of time searching for lost children and answering medical calls for kids who got sick on rides. (If you ever wondered why there are hoses underneath some of the spectacular rides, that's the reason.) It was an intense day but a lucrative one, especially once we got our attendance up.

CHAPTER SIXTEEN
Not Just Another Day in the Park

Each day at the fair had its own special "theme." I'm not sure if anyone other than the staff really cared, but it helped us to plan events and entertainment with specific audiences in mind.

Opening Day was simply that, but it was not simple by any stretch of the imagination. It was chaotic. Everything happened at once, so the pace was frenetic. Last-minute vendors and exhibitors moved in, requiring direction, electric hookups, extra tables and chairs, and a lot of hand-holding. Cars and trucks swarmed the midway as foods, beverages, and supplies were delivered to various vendors. All the inspectors descended onto the fairgrounds, needing assistance or requiring that we move something that encroached on a fire lane, or remove something that was deemed illegal, or tie down a propane tank, or post a sign, or any one of a number of last minute adjustments. As opening time got nearer, the pace quickened, and staff literally ran from place to place so that everything would be ready.

At the height of this fevered pitch, the media showed up, wanting pictures and interviews. Dealing with the media was my job, so I needed to stay cool and collected while my staff ran around like crazy people. Since I also needed to be on the stage for the opening ceremony, I didn't want to be all hot and sweaty, so I tried to stay inside whenever possible. At the last minute, I donned stockings, a dress, and heels so I could look professional for the opening ceremony and the following reception. Putting on pantyhose was not a treat, and I always gave a sigh of relief when the ceremony was over, the gates were open, and the fair was up and running so that I could finally change back into comfortable and cool clothing.

Opening day rarely went smoothly. One year, the first year after we had renovated the fairgrounds, the inspector from the Health Department–Division of Environmental Health created a problem for us. We had installed underground water hook-ups for the carnival and vendors so that we would not have hoses crossing roadways where people could trip on them. Since by Health Department ruling, we needed to test the water for potability before the fair opened, we uncovered the manhole and turned on the faucets to flush the lines. We had done this a hundred times, and although water filled the hole while it was running, once the hoses were connected, within fifteen minutes, the water in the manhole dissipated. Unfortunately, it was during the fifteen minutes when the hole was filled with water that the Health Department showed up. The inspector took one look at the water flooding the manhole and refused to give us a permit to open the fair, stating that the water junction was subject to contamination due to it being under water. We explained what had happened and what would happen in a few minutes, but the health inspector was insistent.

My husband is an engineer, so I called him and asked for advice. He suggested that we get a submersible pump and put it in the manhole. Then, whenever there was water in it, the pump would turn on and get rid of it. The health inspector agreed, so we rented a pump and installed it minutes before the fair was to open. Of course, by that time, there was no longer any water in the hole, and throughout the fair, there was never any water in the hole. But the Health Department was happy, and so was I—until I got the bill for the pump rental.

At that same fair, we were holding a meet-and-greet in the Beer Tent for Henrietta Chamber of Commerce members. Since I was president of the Chamber that year, I was looking forward to the event. I had just finished the opening ceremony and was heading to the Beer Tent when my maintenance supervisor called me to the midway. That year, we had placed the carnival on a newly paved parking lot, and there was a puddle of water on the blacktop under one of the spectacular rides. It hadn't rained for several days, so there was no apparent cause for the water that was seeping up through the pavement. I went to my office and pulled out the infrastructure blueprints, but there were no underground water pipes in that area. However, I knew there were underground springs on the property, and I immediately thought about a possible sinkhole forming under that ride, which would be catastrophic. (You may have noticed that "catastrophe" is my default mode of thinking.)

I called the contractor. He said he had noticed the wet spot during construction, but he had deemed it of no concern. He agreed to come and look at it and again determined that the underlying rock bed was secure and would not crumble. The carnival owner agreed, and I finally breathed a sigh of relief, knowing I had done all I could do. Still, I worried about that spot for the entire fair, and the next year, we moved the carnival to another location.

The second day of the fair was always "Senior Day." I hated Senior Day. I am over sixty-five, so I can say, without prejudice, that seniors can be very demanding and often rude. A lot of them seem to have the attitude that they paid their dues and the world now owed them.

They complained about everything. "It's too far to walk." "It's too hot." "The air conditioner in the Dome is set too low." "The bingo tables have splinters." "Why isn't the fair free for seniors every day?" "Why isn't the fair like it used to be?" "Where's the free food?"

But then I'd see grandparents taking their grandchildren on rides, or playing with them at a ring toss game, or sharing an ice cream cone. Those grandparents were having intergenerational experiences with their grandchildren, and that's what fairs are about: making memories that last. Those images made me hate Senior Day a little less.

Friday was "Youth Day," and on Saturday, we usually recognized first responders or the military and gave them free admission. Sunday was "Family Day" for no particular reason except that we ran out of ideas.

We typically closed at 10 p.m. on the last day of the fair. Sunday was pretty busy, so if there were still a lot of people on the grounds at 10 p.m., we stayed open for another hour or so. After we closed, we did the usual ticket reconciliation and then settled accounts with the carnival while maintenance put away things that were likely to "walk away" during the night. Then it was party time! We ordered pizzas, brought out the beer, and all the staff just kicked back in the Beer Tent and relaxed. In the absence of board members, we let our hair down and laughed about the week and rejoiced that we had all lived through it. At some point, I always made a toast to the best crew a person could have. It was a perfect way to end a grueling week.

CHAPTER SEVENTEEN
I'm From the State Office and I'm Here to Help

In 1999, a tragic thing happened at the Washington County Fair in Greenwich, New York. Waste runoff from the cattle barn seeped into the well water on the fairgrounds, and 1045 people were infected with E. coli bacteria and became very sick. Two people, one a child, died as a result of the illness. Since all county fairs in New York are under the auspices of the New York State Department of Agriculture and Markets, state officials saw the potential for numerous lawsuits, and the New York State Health Department took action.

It decided that all fairs in the state needed to check their drinking water before and during every event held on the fairgrounds to ascertain if there was a sufficient amount of chlorine in it to make it potable. If bacteria were present, they would "eat up" the chlorine, proving that the water was unsafe to drink. This was a *very necessary* procedure for fairgrounds whose water was supplied by wells which could be contaminated and where chlorine could be added if needed. However, the Monroe County Fair had a municipal water supply. I had no say or control over the amount of chlorine present in the water. Still, I was required to test the water in five different locations every day of every event we had on the fairgrounds, and since we were an event center, that made for a lot of testing days.

But the Health Department didn't stop there. In order to test the water, fair boards were required to have a trained and certified "water distribution technician." This meant that someone, that being me, needed to attend a two-day course that cost $375 in order to get the certification, which had to be renewed every four years.

I took Mike, my maintenance supervisor, with me to the class, as I thought it would be good if both of us were certified. There were twenty-seven people enrolled: twenty-five men who laid water pipe for a living, Myke, and me: a sociology major. What I knew about water distribution was that you turned on a faucet and liquid came out of it and was distributed to whatever vessel was placed beneath it. This, apparently, wasn't what the course was about. The instructor started talking, and I was immediately lost.

I long ago decided that if I didn't understand something, I would ask a question. If I looked dumb, so be it. All I wanted to do was pass the damn test at the end of the damn class. The instructor kept talking about "head," which he seemed to think was important. I didn't know what that meant, so without thinking, I raised my hand and asked what "head" meant. The words were barely out of my mouth when I realized what I had just asked in a roomful of men. In two seconds, I turned fifty shades of red. Myke moved his chair slightly farther away from mine and covered his face with his hands, but I could see his shoulders shaking with suppressed laughter. There was a dead silence of maybe three seconds that seemed like a lifetime before the instructor answered. ("Head" means pressure, by the way, at least in fluid mechanics.)

After two days of trying to learn something in which I had no interest, and one night of cramming for the damn test, I passed the damn course. Now, I was certified to put water into a vial, add a tablet to it, and see if the water turned pink.

The Dome and Minett Hall have close to 60,000 linear feet of water pipe. (I'm guesstimating here.) It is also one-quarter of a mile from the water main to the Dome's water junction. In other words, it is a heck of a long way from the water source to the end of the line. Since I was required to take water readings from five different locations, one of those readings needed to be at the end of the line, which was the bathroom in Minett Hall. With 60,000 linear feet of pipe, water sat in the pipes for days, unless we had a show where 5,000 people continually flushed toilets. So, usually, at the start of a show or the day before a show, the water would not turn pink because the chlorine in the pipes had dissipated over the time between events. That meant that I had to turn on as many faucets as possible for a good hour in order to flush the lines so that I could get a chlorine reading. Turning on the outside faucets worked well, except that the parking lot turned into a skating rink in the winter. It also severely diminished the water pressure inside. On a day when we were having a rock concert, we turned on the water outside so that I could test the water. The lead singer in the band happened to be taking a shower at the time. When the water pressure dipped to near nonexistent, he showed up at my office door with a towel wrapped around his waist and shampoo in his hair, wondering, "What the hell happened to the water?" Oops!

So, for the next twelve years, I dutifully tested the water, sometimes spending an hour flushing toilets in the Minett Hall bathroom, hoping for just a hint of pink to show up in the water sample. I also tested the water at my house. Guess what. It didn't turn pink.

Back in 1994, when George Pataki was elected governor of New York, he decided that he wanted to make state government more user-friendly. There was a relatively new law on the books that required nonprofit organizations to file an annual financial report with the New York State Charities Bureau, so he sent his attorney general out to have seminars on how to comply with this law. At these seminars, we were assured that all that was wanted was compliance, and there would be no penalties involved if the report had not been previously filed. After the seminar, I sent for the forms and tried to fill them out. As with most forms issued by the government, a law degree is needed to decipher them. Not having such, I called the attorney general's office to ask a question. User-friendly? The woman who answered the phone was not only rude but also threatening. Anyway, I finally finished the form and sent it to the attorney general, along with a filing fee of $250, which I suspect was the real reason for the new law.

Several months later, I got a nasty letter from the attorney general's office, telling me that I was in violation of the law because I had not sent them the required filing fee and was therefore subject to fines, etc., etc., etc. Since I had the canceled check that proved that I had not only sent the check but that they had cashed it as well, I sent them back a nasty letter telling them how user-friendly they were not.

By chance, we had a show at the Dome, and a local representative from the attorney general's office happened to be an exhibitor, another example of Pataki trying to make government approachable. The guy made the mistake of asking me how things were going, and I gave him an earful. Surprisingly, he took my tale of woe up the chain of command, and I eventually got a letter of apology from the attorney general himself. But after Pataki was voted out of office, I never got a letter from any department in the state that didn't include a threat, even if I was in compliance.

At fair time, we were visited by nearly every regulatory agency in the state and county. The New York State Tax Department came to make sure every vendor had a tax ID number. The agents were always dressed in suits and were very serious. You didn't joke with the tax guys. The Worker's Compensation Board checked to see if everyone had workers comp and to make certain that we had our insurance certificate posted on the wall, which I guess was very important. The Labor Department came to see if we had labor regulations posted on the wall, including minimum wage requirements. (We had a six-foot-by-six-foot bulletin board devoted to these important postings that nobody ever read except for the regulators.) They also made sure there were no minors working. Once, they fined a spa exhibitor because his bored eleven year-old was caught wiping down a hot tub. The County Health Department–Environmental Health Division came to see if the water tuned pink. The County Health Department–Food Protection Division came to check the food vendors but missed Mr. W.'s car trunk filled with raw chicken. The New York State Department of Agriculture and Markets came nearly every day to check the animals to make sure they were healthy and had all their inoculations. The New York State ride inspectors checked the rides. The Liquor Authority made spot checks to see if we were stupid enough to serve alcohol to minors. And the fire marshal came to check fire lanes, fire extinguishers, and propane tanks. From time to time, the FBI showed up to see if any fugitives were working for the carnival as "green help." One year, we had a vendor selling cigarettes, and someone from the Bureau of Alcohol, Tobacco and Firearms came. We also had the New York State Police, who walked through the fair every so often, as well as Monroe County Sheriff's deputies. Since we had our own private security company too, we were probably the safest place on the planet.

All county fairs in New York are under the jurisdiction of the New York State Department of Agriculture and Markets. They are responsible for the health of the animals at the fair. I learned how to work with the vets at Ag and Markets and tried to supply them with whatever would make life easier for them so that they wouldn't make life hard for me. Usually there were one or two animals sent home because they exhibited signs of illness or because their inoculations weren't up to date. When this happened, the exhibitor was invariably unhappy, but I always backed up the vets. But one year, we had a new vet who was a stickler for the rules.

We had a petting zoo booked for the fair, and it was one of our prime attractions. On the evening before the fair was to open, the state vet checked the animals. She found that they did not have the proper inoculations because the New York State requirements had changed that year, and the petting zoo owners were unaware of those changes. She wouldn't allow the petting zoo on the fairgrounds, and she wouldn't budge from her position. I even tried to go over her head, which in retrospect, was not a good thing to do; she took issue with it. I was in a dilemma. I needed the attraction; it had been heavily advertised. Plus, it had cost quite a bit of money, and it was going to be difficult to get a refund as I probably should have recognized and informed the owners of the changes in the regulations.

There was a small strip of land at the edge of our parking lot, right outside the front gate of the fair. The land belonged to our neighbor who had a farm market that adjoined our property. The neighbor happened to be on our board at the time. Since the land was not technically part of the fairgrounds, the vet said she would have no jurisdiction over the animals if we were to place them there. Our neighbor agreed to the plan, and we arrived at a compromise. It wasn't ideal, but it solved the problem.

Because we had animals at the fair, we also had picketers from PETA. I did not want any confrontations, so I cautioned my staff not to interact with them. For my part, I always made it a point to greet the picketers and to treat them with respect. I wanted them to be able to protest in safety, so I showed them where they could march that would keep them out of the way of motor vehicle traffic. The picketers were always grateful for my lack of animosity and for my concern, and as a result, we never had any trouble, and we kept the picketing out of the news.

I did have a problem with the SPCA (Society for the Prevention of Cruelty to Animals), however. One year, the livestock superintendent showed up in my office. He was quite upset because an animal control officer had come to the barn and complained that farm animals had no business being at fairs. He felt it was unhealthy for them, and since the SPCA was a county organization and we were in Monroe County, he believed he had the authority to order that the animals be sent home. I contacted the doctor at Ag and Markets who made it clear to the SPCA that their organization had no jurisdiction at fairs and that the animals were being cared for quite well and were being monitored by state veterinarians. Although it was beastly hot outside, the animals were housed in an air-conditioned, scrupulously clean barn—conditions that were far better than what the staff was enduring. Perhaps the SPCA should have sent us home instead. (Yes, please.) It was a difficult confrontation that left both the officials at the SPCA and me with lingering hard feelings.

Every year, we had a ceremony on opening day of the fair. The press usually covered the event, and we tried to time it so we made the five or six o'clock news. I always sent passes to all local and county officials, inviting them to attend, and I asked key members of the town and county to sit on the dais and to say a few words. One year, no one turned up for the opening ceremony except for the elected officials, and they all insisted on sitting on the stage. We gave our speeches to empty chairs. That was not one of my finest hours.

I think it was at my third fair when the opening ceremony really went awry. I asked a high-ranking county official to attend and invited him to speak. Although I had never met him, I heard through the grapevine that he didn't like me, probably because I wasn't a member of his political party. Although I not only sent him a pass to get into the fair but also a map and directions as to where to park, from what I was able to piece together after the fact, he allegedly couldn't find his parking spot and he forgot his entrance pass. The kids who were parking the cars had no idea who he was and directed him to park quite far from the entrance. Since he was late to begin with, this made him very late. I had no idea this was happening, and held up the opening ceremony for forty-five minutes while I waited for him. Finally, members of the county legislature insisted that I start because there was a legislative meeting that night that they needed to attend. So, I reluctantly began the proceedings and was about ten minutes into it when the county official, who was not happy that I had started without him, arrived.

If he disliked me before, this fiasco really sealed the deal. I spent the next few years trying to thwart the county's attempts to gain control of our privately owned fairgrounds. A nasty and very public campaign was orchestrated against the Fair Association and me—a strategy that had worked with several other entities that the county wanted under its auspices. With the cooperation of town officials, we were issued violations that came with hefty fines on minute matters. For example, we were told we were in violation because there was no sign on the door to the boiler room that said NO ADMITTANCE. We were in violation because a fire hydrant was painted red instead of yellow. We were in violation because we had boxes stored under a staircase. Moreover, the town now had a new requirement that we get permits for every outdoor event, like RV shows.

I was taken to court personally rather than as director of the Fair Association, clandestine meetings were held with rogue board members who were urged to advocate selling the fairgrounds to the county, and a comprehensive media campaign painted the Fair Association and me in a horrible light. Still, the Fair Association held its ground, and the fair remained a private, nonprofit corporation. The turnaround came when our lawyer threatened to sue the town for unequal enforcement of the law as well as for civil rights violations. It was a very stressful time for the board and for me, but I'm proud that we stood up to the pressure. I've had many people tell me that they couldn't believe we succeeded. Needless to say, I was very relieved when the official finally left office.

One of the things that the town tried to do during this period was to require that we get permits for tents during the fair. Since we used many tents, the cost would have been prohibitive. I contacted the attorney at Ag and Markets who called the town's attorney and informed him that the town could not charge any permitting fees during the county fair as it was prohibited by law. It was gamesmanship at this point, and I always needed to be one move ahead.

Working with town code enforcement was always interesting. Depending on who was working on any particular day, cars parked on the fairgrounds for shows were randomly ticketed. Often, things were said in the press that were quite derogatory, and I always seemed to be at odds with the head of code enforcement, despite my attempts to be in compliance with everything. I think my problems with him stemmed from the fact that he had once held my job before he was asked to step down. Finally, I decided to meet with the man to see if we had any common ground. At the meeting, I casually mentioned that I was Italian, knowing that he was as well, and it was as if the sun suddenly shone on a gloomy day.

"Why didn't you tell me?" he said, grasping my hand. "We have to stick together."

From that time on, I had an ally in the town. If I had a problem, he was quick to fix it; if he had a problem, he let me know so that I could fix it before it went public. I found the arrangement very strange but pragmatic, and it made my life a heck of a lot easier than before.

I sorely needed an ally in the town. The supervisor and I did not have a warm relationship. In fact, whenever I had to see him on any matter, I could feel my stomach clenching because I knew I was in for either a tongue lashing or at best, a condescending attitude. If he had a problem with anything, I frequently read about it in the press before there was any face-to-face discussion on the matter. When he eventually left office, the new supervisor and I got along wonderfully. But even with this new supervisor, I still got nervous flutters in my stomach every time I sat in his outer office waiting to see him. I guess the body remembers even when the mind knows otherwise.

Another entity that was often frustrating and difficult to deal with was the New York State Liquor Authority. We had a permanent license to sell beer and wine at our concession stand in the Dome. During concerts, especially country concerts, we wanted to have several kiosks around the Dome to handle the crowds that wanted beer, thus increasing our revenue and eliminating the lines that frequently blocked the sightline of other concert-goers. This meant that we had to apply for temporary licenses for every kiosk every time we had a concert. Each temporary license, of course, cost money. It seemed to be a silly regulation. If we were licensed to sell beer, why did we need a separate license to sell beer twenty feet away from the original licensed location? The Liquor Authority admitted that there wasn't anything in the law that specifically dealt with facilities like ours, but they nevertheless continued to require that we have numerous licenses. But getting these licenses was always a hassle. If I tried to be efficient and send in the applications well ahead of when they were needed, they would be put aside and often lost. If I sent them too late, I was in danger of never getting them in time. As a result, I spent a lot of time on the phone with the Liquor Authority, trying to track down our applications.

The Environmental Protection Agency created several unpleasant experiences for us. As I mentioned, the Dome and Minett Hall were originally built as ice arenas. There were pipes under the concrete floor that held anti-freeze in the form of ethylene glycol. As the years passed, the pipes corroded and began to leak. Eventually, the anti-freeze found its way to the surface of the floor. We discovered the pink liquid bubbling through the floor in Minett Hall on the morning we were holding a dog show in that building. Ethylene glycol is extremely toxic to animals as well as being very attractive to them because of its sweet taste. (Some states are now adding a bittering agent to it.) I had visions of numerous lawsuits, and I foresaw newspaper headlines that said things like: SHOW DOGS GO TO THE BIG SHOW AFTER DOME CENTER POISONING. So, we blocked off a portion of the floor, and after the show was over, we called in a contractor to jackhammer that area and to pump the anti-freeze out of all the pipes in the building. This required an inspection by the EPA and then disposal of the anti-freeze. The cost of that operation was monumental.

But it was cheap compared with our next experience. When we were in the process of selling a parcel of our land to a supermarket chain, we were required to have an environmental inspection. The inspectors discovered an old gas tank that was buried under the parking lot. It had been there for years and had leaked gasoline into the soil. This necessitated that we call in a contractor to dig up the tank and all the soil surrounding it, which created a hole the size of Rhode Island. The contractor kept testing the soil to see how far the gasoline had traveled, and the hole kept getting bigger. This was a problem because I was told that the contaminated soil had to be trucked to Arizona in order for it to be disposed of properly and that we were responsible for the trucking costs. The more they dug, the more dollar signs I saw. Finally, it was determined that there was still some soil contamination, but because the soil was densely packed clay, the gasoline wasn't really going to travel any further. (That was the only time I was grateful for the clay soil.) A special kind of anaerobic bacteria was placed in the hole, and then the hole was backfilled with clean soil that we had to purchase. The bacteria would eat up the remaining gasoline, and the EPA was happy. That little episode made the ethylene glycol cleanup seem like a bargain.

As I mentioned before, we had a small creek running through our property. It ran along the edge of the parking lot and bordered the meadow that would become the new motorsport track. The previous executive director had wanted to host a balloon rally there, so he obtained a culvert that was placed in the creek. Then he built a wooden bridge over the culvert so people and cars could get into the meadow. He didn't ask anybody; he just did it. Since it had been there for years before I came to the fairgrounds, we continued to use it. Once we decided to build the track in the meadow, we wanted to get the competing cars into the track area without having to drive through the fair to get to the makeshift bridge. We determined that a small, five-foot bridge that led directly from the parking lot to the track would do the trick. However, the creek was a dedicated waterway, so we needed to have an environmental study in order to build it. The upshot was that it would cost us $100,000 to build this five-foot bridge across the inch of water in the creek. We didn't do it.

All in all, my experiences with government at all levels were not very positive. When I first came to the fair, I naively felt that if I were honest and straightforward with our lawmakers, they would do the right thing and help us to accomplish our goal of becoming a community center and asset. That was before I was introduced to hidden agendas, other agendas, political agendas, old grievances, new grievances, personality differences, differences of opinion, old ways of thinking, new ways of thinking, bureaucratic ways of thinking, apathy, and lethargy. I always tried to follow the law, but that turned out to be very costly. Maybe I should have taken a cue from my predecessor and asked for forgiveness rather than for permission.

That Damn Roof!

I had a love/hate relationship with the fairgrounds. I loved the fair. I loved the shows we had at the fairgrounds. I loved the challenge of being in the event industry. The fairgrounds became my second home, and I embraced all the quirks inherent to buildings erected in the 1970s.

For example, the HVAC system was a constant source of frustration as the whole system had been cobbled together from parts of the original ice-making equipment. The offices had no central heating or cooling so, until we got a new boiler system, we huddled around space heaters in the winter and sweltered in the summer.

Although the heating and cooling system in the Dome was somewhat spotty, what worked well was the ventilation system. It blew all odors directly into my office. This was especially evident when we hosted the Pet Expo. The smell of elephant dung is not something easily forgotten. Other odors also bombarded me: manure from the livestock barn during the fair, mulch from the garden show, car exhaust from car shows, propane from the forklifts, and one day, the very strong odor of gasoline. My brain was somewhat foggy from the fumes as I stumbled into the Dome in search of the source of the odor. I found that one of my maintenance workers was trying to remove motor oil from the Dome floor by using gasoline as a solvent. It was working, but the whole building was full of gasoline fumes, and I had visions of it blowing up, along with all of us. I ordered him to stop and to open every door until the smell dissipated. It was a freezing cold day in March, so the directive was not greeted with much enthusiasm. Since it was my first week as executive director of the Fair Association, I'm sure my maintenance staff thought I was just being hysterical.

But the biggest source of my frustration was that damn roof. As I mentioned previously, the Dome was built as a prototype of the domed structures that became popular in the 1970s, but the design did not work well in Upstate New York.

The Dome's roof was built with a wooden deck, swathed in foam insulation, and covered with a neoprene membrane. Around the perimeter was a wooden parapet, also known as a Yankee gutter, which supported the opaque, Plexiglas windows that also encircled the building. The roof was built on springs so that it could actually move up and down as the weight of snow accumulated on it. It was an engineering marvel. Too bad it didn't work.

In the winter, several things happened. Snow fell on the roof. Since the heat was on inside the building and warm air rises, the internal heat would begin to melt the snow, which would then avalanche off the roof, tearing the membrane and wiping out the lightning rods that surrounded the roof. It sounded like an earthquake if you were inside the Dome when the snow gave way. But the avalanched snow didn't just fall to the ground. It accumulated on the parapet where it formed huge ice sculptures, like giant waves that pointed skyward. This added a great deal of weight to the parapet that was not built for such. As luck would have it, most of those waves formed over the exit doors. Eventually the snow waves began to melt and crash to the ground. We tried to keep the doorways clear, but it was a losing battle. I watched many exhibitors run for their lives as snow and ice cascaded around them.

One year, we had an exceptionally bad winter with two major snowstorms in the course of a week. I had been at the fairgrounds for several years, and I had never seen anything like it. The roof flexed as it was designed to do, but it reached its limit. The snow load was just too great.

My maintenance supervisor called me into the Dome. The windows on the south side of the building were bowing outward because the load on the sagging parapet could no longer hold them in place. We called a roofing company that brought in an excavator to remove the snow from the parapet. It was a dangerous job because snow could avalanche and bury both the excavator and the excavator operator.

I was at a meeting with a potential fair sponsor while the snow was being removed from the parapet. We had tried to get an appointment with this business for months, so there was no way I was going to cancel the meeting despite the inopportune timing. If we succeeded, it would mean a lot of money for the fair. In the middle of the negotiations, my marketing director's cell phone rang. He excused himself to answer the call but returned a minute later and handed me his phone. My secretary was calling, and she was nearly hysterical.

"It's bad! It's really bad, Fran! You need to come back!" she shouted, loudly enough for the whole room to hear.

Hysteria was not exactly the message I wanted to convey to a potential sponsor, so I calmly explained that we had a roof issue with which I needed to deal when I returned to the Dome.

But my secretary was right. It was bad. In the course of removing the snow, the parapet had collapsed, causing the windows to tumble out onto the ground below. Now, we had a real problem. With part of the support no longer supporting anything, we didn't know whether the roof was still structurally sound. This meant calling in a structural engineer who was flummoxed because domes were so rare that no one knew exactly what the load-bearing parameters actually were. After much angst, the Dome was deemed safe, and our scheduled gun show went off as planned.

When the parapet collapsed, the press arrived at the Dome before I did, having been called by a nosy neighbor who delighted whenever a calamity arose at the fairgrounds. I begged the TV reporter not to say that the Dome *roof* had collapsed, as it wasn't really the roof that was the problem. It was the parapet. But of course the lead was, "DOME ROOF COLLAPSES," followed by derogatory comments from the town supervisor and the code enforcement officer about the state of the fairgrounds. Despite the bad publicity, or probably because of it, the gun show had its biggest attendance in history, and the promoters asked if I could arrange for that kind of publicity before all of their shows.

With the roofing company's aerial excavation, the engineering inspections, the new windows that were anything but standard, and the re-building of the parapet, the bill for that little incident was exorbitant. So of course, I submitted it to our insurance company, which of course, refused to pay it because our policy "didn't cover gutters." Reversing the directions I gave to the reporter about not saying that *the roof* had collapsed, I argued with the insurance company that the parapet was not actually a gutter in the usual sense of the word but was actually an integral part of the roof system. It took months and several insurance inspections before the insurance company paid, and we were finally able to get rid of the ugly plywood that covered the hole where the Dome windows had been and to begin repairs on that damn roof.

Thereafter, whenever we had any significant snowfall, I had members of my maintenance staff go up in the bucket of our forklift and shovel the snow off the roof. With my acrophobia, this was a hair-raising ordeal for me as well as for the poor guys who actually had to do the work in the middle of a blizzard. But we never again had that particular problem with that damn roof.

Every time the snow avalanched off the roof and tore a hole in the membrane, the roof leaked at the site of the hole. Sometimes the hole was so big that it was like a waterfall. We were constantly berated by angry exhibitors because of a leak that suddenly sprang up, dripping water and wet snow onto their heads or exhibits. I hated getting those calls because there was nothing we could do to fix the problems until spring. Then the leaks would be repaired, but there would be black patches on the white membrane where the bandages had been placed. I finally decided we needed to paint the roof, as it was looking pretty spotty. That was not an easy proposition. First of all, we needed to use a special paint that cost $200 a gallon. Then the roof had to be prepared so the paint would stick to the membrane. When all was said and done, it would cost $50,000 to paint that damn roof.

We hired a painting company, and they began work. One day, I noticed that one of the workers was on the roof without a safety harness. As the surface was quite slippery with wet paint, he was having fun sliding down the slope of it. I yelled at him about needing a safety harness, but he just shrugged and laughed. Fifteen minutes later, he fell off that damn roof, and broke his arm.

There is a law in New York State called the Scaffold Law that was enacted in 1895. It states that if anyone falls from a height while on your property, you, as the property owner, have absolute liability. So even though the painter worked for a sub-contractor who had workers' compensation, and even though he was required by his company to wear a safety harness that was actually attached to the top of the roof, and even though I had warned him that he needed a safety harness, we were still liable and ended up being sued. That damn roof!

CHAPTER NINETEEN

Show Business—
There's Nothing Like It

Like most fairgrounds, we needed off-season business to be able to pay for the fair, so shows at the event center were crucial to our mission of "building community through the advancement of youth, agriculture, and technology."

Our shows were very diverse. One year on the same weekend, we had a motorcycle swap meet in Minett Hall and a flower show in the Dome. An elderly Catholic priest, who had intended to go to the flower show, accidentally got in line for the swap meet. He was amazed at how excited the motorcyclists appeared to be about flowers before he realized he was in the wrong line.

But the diversity made the business exciting. Each week, we shifted gears to accommodate the very different needs of our clients. Sometimes, the shifts took funny turns, especially the week we hosted a Catholic retreat that was immediately followed by a labor union party. The retreat was especially interesting. A nationally known, conservative Catholic priest did a three-day prayer and reflection event that we held in the Dome. Each day, the priest had over a thousand people come to listen to him preach. In one of our small rooms, he set up a chapel where the Blessed Sacrament was exposed so that people could come to worship there.

But some very strange things began to happen shortly after the group moved in. First, the drains backed up, causing floods in the bathrooms and in the concession stands. It wasn't raining, so there was no reason for this to have occurred. We called in Roto-Rooter and got the lines open. Then, three hours before the start of the first sermon, all the electricity went off in the building—again for no apparent reason. As we scurried around, trying to locate enough generators to get us up and running, we were told by the organizers that they were used to strange things happening whenever Father spoke. They were convinced that Satan didn't want him to preach. This freaked out all of us. Fortunately, the local utility company came through, and the lights came back on just before we were ready to open the doors.

One afternoon, I had a little free time, so I decided to listen to one of the priest's sermons. As a not-so-conservative Catholic woman who might have been a priest if given the opportunity, I found myself getting more and more angry as I listened to him. He was against any form of birth control, against women becoming priests, and he felt that a woman should be in the home, not in the workplace. I came to believe that it wasn't Satan who didn't want Father to preach; it was most likely God Herself who was trying to make a point!

The day after the retreat, we hosted a labor union party. The "chapel" became a bar, and the clientele was vastly different from those who had come for a day of prayer and reflection. I chuckled as I stopped myself from making the sign of the cross as I walked by the chapel/bar.

One of our most enduring shows was the motorcycle swap meet. We held one or two every year, and I never had any kind of problem with them. I found the exhibitors and customers to be polite and friendly, and although the neighbors weren't too thrilled with the noise of the bikes, the show was an easy one to host. However, one year, our first responders were up in arms. There was a rumor that the president of the Hell's Angels had been invited to speak. This was during a particularly trying time when there had been a number of incidents of bad blood among several motorcycle brotherhoods, including a couple of murders, and the intelligence on the street was that having the president of the Hell's Angels at the show was going to be dangerous.

I had meetings with the FBI, the Sheriff's Department, and town officials, and all of them wanted me to cancel the show. But we had a long-standing contract with the show promoter, and I refused. Came the day of the show and we had more law enforcement people than we had customers. We had undercover FBI agents, sheriff's deputies, both uniformed and under cover, police on motorcycles, police on foot, and police on horseback. The Monroe County Sheriff, himself a biker, actually showed up. Who didn't show up was the president of the Hell's Angels. It was the most peaceful show we ever had.

Having concerts was big business for us, but I always had mixed feelings about them. The country concerts were great. People were mellow and polite, and there was usually a family atmosphere, although we did sell a lot of beer, especially when the concert coincided with St. Patrick's Day.

We had two country concerts a year that were sponsored by a local radio station. They used a simple, acoustic format with several stars on stage who took turns singing. We had some pretty big-name stars including Big & Rich, Blake Shelton, Carrie Underwood, Rachael Wilson, Kellie Pickler, and Tanya Tucker, to name a few. One year, my events director brought Joe Nichols into the office to introduce him. At the time, I really wasn't into country music, so his name meant nothing to me. I think I ruined his day when I asked him who he was. Oh well, at least I didn't turn off the water on him while he was showering.

When you're in the fair business, it's almost sacrilegious to say you don't like country music, but I really hated it. At every fair convention or zone meeting, country music was all that was played, and I found it boring and repetitious. At one such meeting, there was a Tammy Wynette cover band that "entertained" us after dinner. It was so depressing with the dog dying, and the husband cheating, and the trailer burning down. If I never heard another country song, it was okay with me. However, that year, every radio station in Rochester, except for the country stations, started playing Christmas music even before Thanksgiving. When I couldn't tolerate one more version of "I'll be Home for Christmas," I reluctantly tuned into the country station. By the end of the holiday season, I was a country music convert, which helped me to finally fit in at fair events as well as to recognize the songs played at our country concerts.

Rock concerts were different animals entirely—different clientele, different social dynamic, different vibe. I remember my first one. The Foo Fighters, Blink 182, and Primus were on their way up and were openers for Bush. The concert was held at the end of April. I previously mentioned our antiquated HVAC system. It was such that there was either heat or air conditioning. There was no way there could be both. We usually made the conversion to air in late May to coincide with Rochester's May 21st to May 23rd spring, which is followed immediately by summer. April in Rochester is still winter.

The concert was a sell-out, and the Dome floor was packed. Since there was no air conditioning, with the stage lights and the dancing in the mosh pit, the temperature in the Dome rapidly rose to the low 90s. Once I was certain that the event was running smoothly, I went up to the press box to observe what was happening on the show floor. Because of the heat and all the people, there was so much humidity in the air that every surface around the press box was dripping with condensation, and there was actually fog drifting over the gyrating bodies below me. The Dome was dark except for the stage lights that were pulsing red, and the audience crowded the stage, arms in the air, their fists pounding toward the source of the chaotic sound. I could feel the boom of the bass vibrating through my body, and I remember thinking that this must be what hell is like.

We hosted Bush again in the mid-2000s, this time with an outdoor concert on our newly renovated grounds. Four bands opened for Bush, so it was a great Sunday afternoon of music in a brand new festival setting. Unfortunately, the language that the bands used was not exactly G-rated, and although the music didn't seem to be overly loud at the festival site, there was one speaker that apparently aimed the sound directly into the living rooms of the people who lived across the street from the fairgrounds. These people were not pleased with the music or the lyrics and began calling, not only the fairgrounds, but also the town supervisor, code enforcement, the police, and even the office of the county executive. I was not a popular person with our neighbors for months following that concert.

Worrier that I am, I obsessed over the rock concerts. We invariably had a fight or two, but security was tight, and fights were stopped pretty quickly. Mosh pits were new, and there were the inevitable injuries, mostly caused by stupidity. Although the injuries and incidents were never severe, I was always a nervous wreck before and during the concerts. I always prayed for rain so that people wouldn't linger in the parking lot after the shows, which is when and where fights escalated.

The thing that always amazed me and, I must admit, bothered me, was how easily the people coming to concerts submitted to security checks. They willingly raised their arms for a pat-down or metal scan and didn't seem to mind having their backpacks and purses searched. I grew up at a time when being searched was unheard of—as well as against the law—and it made me uncomfortable to see this docile compliance. Of course, these concerts were post 9/11, and people said they would rather be searched than feel unsafe at a concert where searches weren't conducted.

The Marilyn Manson concert was one that really concerned me. I expected it to be pretty wild; instead, the kids were well-behaved and very docile. They came dressed in Goth clothing and makeup, picked a spot on the floor, and pretty much stayed put. They didn't even go to the concession stands.

The concert was held on a very cold night, and most of the kids didn't have coats or sweaters. They were mostly young teens who had to wait for rides home. For security's sake, we always swept everyone out the doors of the building as soon as the concert ended, but as I watched those kids freezing their buns off, my maternal instinct crept in, and I let them back inside to keep warm. The kids huddled on the floor and were grateful and polite. Despite the screams from my security guards, it was the right call.

A concert that we didn't have caused us more trouble than

concerts we did have. A promoter approached us about hosting a nationally famous rap artist. I was somewhat apprehensive about this performance because gun violence seemed to follow in the wake of concerts by this particular artist. However, I knew it would be good business for us and potentially open up our venue for other national acts of this caliber, so I put my reservations aside, and we signed the contract with the promoter.

We required all show promoters to provide us with certificates of insurance that named the Monroe County Fair Association as additionally insured, so if something went wrong and we were sued, we would be covered under the promoter's insurance before our own kicked in. The certificate was due within days of the signing of the contract, but two days before the date of the rap concert, I still didn't have proof of insurance from the promoter. Despite repeated phone calls to him, he kept stalling.

Then our sound technician called me. He said he hadn't been paid his required deposit for providing sound for the show, and unless he was paid in full before the start of the concert, he would refuse to allow us to open the doors. Meanwhile, reports of gunfire at the artist's concerts continued to be reported in the press.

I sent my events director to Syracuse for reconnaissance since the rapper was playing a concert at a venue there. I asked her to assess the safety of the show and also to confront the promoter and to obtain both the required certificate of insurance and the money needed for the sound technician. With ticket sales, the promoter should have had cash available. When my events director returned, she was pretty negative about the concert. She said that shots had been fired from a car as people were leaving the concert facility, and the gunfire had continued and spread to several blocks in the surrounding area. News reports confirmed this. Moreover, she had been unsuccessful in obtaining both the money and the insurance certificate.

At that point, even though it was only twenty-four hours until show time, I canceled the concert. I knew there were going to be a lot of upset people, but with the advance announcement, I thought it would be easier to handle a few people at a time who wanted refunds. If 3,000 people showed up expecting to see a concert only to find locked doors and a dark facility, we could have a riot on our hands.

The concert promoter was livid and wanted to shift the blame for the cancellation in order to take the heat off himself, so he contacted a local radio station and went live on the air, blaming us for canceling the concert. The DJ called me, and in real time, I had to explain why I had done what I did. Fortunately, the evidence of the promoter's incompetence was compelling, and the blame quickly shifted back to him. (It was after this fiasco that I found that a wine glass, or two, of Amaretto was a good way to cope with the trials of being a facility manager.)

We were pretty much off the hook, but the drama didn't end there. Tickets were sold in a variety of venues, including ours, although we probably sold only about twenty or thirty of them. Ticket holders were instructed to return to their points of purchase in order to get refunds. Since we hadn't kept records as to who had purchased tickets from us, we were stuck when a number of people, who had actually purchased tickets elsewhere, came to us for refunds. It cost us several hundred dollars before all the dust had settled.

Not all of our concerts had this degree of drama. Some bands performed successfully and returned for repeat concerts. The Insane Clown Posse was booked three times. My maintenance staff hated that group because they sprayed their audiences with Fanta soda, which made a god-awful, sticky mess to clean up.

Actually, the aftermath of any concert was the stuff of nightmares. Picture the havoc in your living room on Christmas morning after all the presents have been opened, and then multiply that mess by 25,000. There were cups, cans, and paper plates everywhere, along with strewn popcorn from discarded boxes, confetti, half-eaten hot dogs, gobs of melted cheese from nachos, pools of spilled beer, and stray pieces of clothing, usually bras. As I said before, my maintenance crew was a marvel.

The problem that we always had with concerts was that the acoustics in the Dome were dreadful. It was built as an ice arena, not as a music hall. Sound bounced off the walls and ceiling, so it was impossible to hear more than just echoes or, if you were in a dead zone, nothing at all. We finally found a sound company that corrected the problem by using a computer program to direct the sound. We always urged promoters to use that company. It was pricey, but the results were fantastic. Sometimes, a promoter would decide he knew better than we did, and he would book another sound company, which always had disastrous results. Then the concert reviews were awful, which gave the Dome a bad name.

One thing that I did learn as a result of the concerts was to identify the smell of marijuana. Although I went to college in the 60s, I guess I hung out with the wrong (or the right) people, depending on your point of view. I remember when my daughter was a teenager, I would often smell something coming from her bathroom and tell her that it smelled like marijuana. She would laugh and show me that it was actually vanilla-scented body splash. I had no clue what marijuana smelled like except I was told that it smelled sweet, which vanilla body splash definitely does. However, after breathing in the fumes from multiple concerts, I will never again mistake vanilla for marijuana.

We did a number of teen dances, and often smelled marijuana at them, as well. We always marveled at the clothes, or lack of same, in which the girls came to the dances. They were young teens, yet many were dressed quite scantily or provocatively, and several times a night, we interrupted lap dances or bathroom trysts. Eventually, rival groups came to the dances, and when neither the police nor we could control the fighting, the police strongly "suggested" that we discontinue them. I always felt sad about that. They started out so positively and ended so badly.

My favorite show of all was Gardenscape. It was held in late March when everyone was thinking spring yet knowing spring was still a month or two away. Landscape companies built elaborate gardens in the Dome, complete with ponds and fountains and cabins. The smell of flowers permeated the buildings (as did the smell of mulch, which wasn't quite as pleasant.) My favorite time was after the show closed for the night. Then with the lights turned low, I could stroll by myself through the gardens and enjoy that touch of summer. It was magical.

The Outdoor Sportsmen's show was a very popular event with some people and not so much with others. We always had animal rights protesters. One year, some protester dumped red fox urine around one of the pillars in the Dome lobby. Fox urine is used by gardeners to deter deer and rabbits, and it smells like skunk. The odor was so strong that, with our eyes streaming, we had to evacuate the building until it dissipated.

The Outdoor Sportsmen's Show was always held in early March, which is not a great time weather-wise in Rochester. One move-in day, I awoke to find that we were in the middle of a winter nor'easter. The snow was falling so hard that I could barely see out the window, but, despite the weather, I was certain that my maintenance staff would be on-hand to assist the promoters. I was also certain that the crew would have plowed the driveway in from the main road so that trucks could get to the Dome to unload.

I decided that I needed to be at work to make sure everything went as planned, so I followed behind a snowplow for the eight-mile drive from my home to the fairgrounds. It usually took fifteen minutes. That day, it took an hour, and I breathed a sigh of relief when I finally spotted the marquee that marked the entrance to the facility. I turned off the road into the driveway and ran smack dab into two feet of snow, burying my small car.

It was about a quarter-mile from the marquee to my office, so I figured I could leave my car where it was and walk to the building. I got out of the car. It was snowing so hard that I could see only a foot or so ahead of me, and the wind was blowing the snow sideways at about forty miles per hour across the open track area to my right. In order to navigate the accumulated snow, I had to lift my leg almost to waist level with every step. I got about twenty feet from my car, and with the wind, the cold, and the exertion, I could scarcely breathe. Unless I got back to my car, I was going to die of a heart attack if not from exposure.

I turned back and struggled to my Subaru. Thankfully, it was red. If it had been white, I never would have found it. I turned on the heat so I could thaw. This immediately caused the windshield to totally fog, so I opened the side windows to clear the obscured windshield, although I couldn't see anything but snow anyway, so I have no idea why I did this. At that moment, a snowplow came through on the road directly behind me and dumped an additional two feet of snow and slush onto my car and through my open car windows. Now, I was not only cold but also wet. I said some very un-nice things.

Using my cell phone, I finally reached my maintenance supervisor. He had made it into work, but he couldn't get to the snow plow because it was in one of the front buildings that was snowed in. He needed a snow plow in order to get to the snow plow and ultimately, to get to me. That's when the battery on my car died.

I have to add here that my car had been quirky from the time I drove it out of the dealer's lot. It had an unidentifiable electrical drain, so it was prone to having frequent bouts of "dead batteryitis." It happened so frequently that I finally started storing a battery pack in the trunk of my car so that I could recharge the battery myself. The electrical drain also caused several other anomalies. I could be driving along and suddenly the car doors would unlock and re-lock, or the lights would flash. Most aggravating was when the car's alarm system would randomly blare, usually when I was in the middle of heavy traffic on the expressway or driving through a part of the city where remaining inconspicuous was always a good idea. Of course, whenever I took the car into the dealer to be checked, it behaved beautifully. I strongly suspected that the car was haunted, so I wasn't surprised when the battery died in the middle of the storm. I wasn't surprised, but I was damned annoyed at the car's perversity.

My daughter was seriously dating a guy who worked near the Dome. She called him, and he got a bunch of his co-workers together who came out *en masse* to rescue me. They dug out my car, gave my battery a jump, and followed me as I tried to make it to their parking lot. The snow was coming down so quickly that even with the snow plows running, there was still at least a foot of snow on the main roads. My car was a sporty Subaru SVX, which sat very low to the ground, and even with all-wheel drive, I couldn't negotiate that amount of snow. My rescuers pulled me out of the snow three times before we actually arrived at their place of business that was less than a mile down the road.

I spent a few hours in their conference room, trying to thaw and dry out and waiting for the snow to let up. When the snow still hadn't stopped by 2:00 p.m., I followed my daughter's boyfriend (who is now my son-in-law) to his apartment. It was a typical bachelor apartment, meaning he had no food except for a can of tomato soup, which we mixed with water and ate with no crackers. Then I tried to get home. I got stuck several more times, including in my own driveway. I eventually entered my house ten hours after I had left it, having accomplished nothing except driving to and from work.

The next day was bright and sunny, and the Sportsmen's show moved in, even though we were still under a state of emergency. That was the first of the storms that caused the roof collapse (excuse me, parapet collapse) problem.

Our most highly attended shows were the gun shows that we held four or five times a year. Although not popular with everyone, they were very well run and controlled, at least inside. I have no idea what was going on in the parking lot.

Guns were checked for bullets before they were allowed into the facility, and their triggers were tied. That worked quite well until one security guard missed seeing a bullet that was still in a gun's chamber. The gun fired, slamming the bullet into the concrete floor just outside my office, which scared the hell out of me, not to mention the security guard and the people who happened to be lined up at the ticket booth. Fortunately, the bullet didn't ricochet, which could have been disastrous. Thereafter, the show provided sand traps that would slow the momentum of any stray bullets.

I remember my first gun show. I was walking the exhibit floor when I caught something out of the corner of my eye. When I turned, there was a man pointing a rather large rifle at me. I stopped dead (not literally) in my tracks, and the man suddenly realized the implications of what he was doing and lowered the gun. He looked abashed and was quite apologetic as he noticed my shaking hands and pale face.

One of the idiosyncrasies of the gun show was that at every show, some guy would defecate on the floor of the men's bathroom and then smear the feces on the walls of the stall. We dubbed the man "The Mad Shitter" and did everything we could to catch him. We never did find out who he was.

Another of our shows came about as a result of our association with Joanne Cercone, who did so much for us during the fair. She was the organizer of the Mrs. New York America Pageant. I had worked with Joanne for a number of years when I asked her to sing the National Anthem at one of our annual meetings. When the meeting was over, I could tell she was upset about something. She said she had lost her venue for the Mrs. New York America Pageant and feared she would have to cancel the show.

After giving it some thought, I offered to hold the pageant at the Dome. I let her use the facility for free, hoping we could regain some of our losses through concession sales. I also hoped it would be a good promotional tool that would demonstrate to other organizers that we were capable of hosting such an event.

We held the pageant for a number of years, and I have to say that it was a trip. Joanne moved in two weeks before the show and pretty much took over the Dome with rehearsals, sound checks, costume fittings, and catered meals for the cast and crew. If Kirstie from the horse arena was a Class A scrounger, Joanne was right up there with her. She always got the elaborate repasts, along with prizes for the contestants, donated. It was a thing of wonder.

One year, Joanne decided that I needed to go on stage during the pageant so I could be recognized as a supporter of the event. To say I was reluctant to do this would be an understatement. I was used to public appearances, so it wasn't that I was shy about going on stage. But going on stage with a group of the most beautiful women in New York State was another thing entirely. My confidence level was not that great, and although I dressed in my most sparkly outfit, I felt totally inadequate, especially when I had to take a picture with the winners. My ego always took a blow.

Lidia Szczepanowski, Mrs. New York America 2006 (left)
and me (right)

But I enjoyed meeting the contestants and trying to figure out who would win. Because Joanne stipulated that promoting the Monroe County Fair was one of the winner's duties, I got to know and to like most of those women. They certainly added a bit of glamour to our fair.

Kathy Kasprak, Mrs. New York America 2000 crowns Christine Countryman (2001)

CHAPTER TWENTY

Money! Money! Money!

The Monroe County Fair Association is a nonprofit corporation, and we were always trying to earn money to make ends meet. The overhead on the facility was scandalous. Since there was no insulation anywhere, heating and cooling the building cost a small fortune. Because we were a fair, insurance costs were exorbitant and added to the budgeting nightmare. With payroll and depreciation added, expenses were high even before we included anything else, like maintenance costs, which were considerable since the buildings were over twenty-five years old.

We tried lots of fundraisers over the years. We had membership drives, dinners, cruise nights, skating parties, Halloween parties, and the aforementioned Great Cow Caper. But like the Cow Caper, I seemed to be one of the few people who actually supported our fundraisers.

One year, I saw an ad for customized, fair-themed, tapestried throw blankets that would include our fair's name. They were pretty and colorful, and I just knew our board members would support the cause, so I ordered twenty-five, a minimal order. Everyone on my Christmas list got a blanket that year, and the board and staff probably bought five more. The rest we used as door prizes for various events over the next seven years.

Undaunted, I had another idea. We were selling a portion of the fairgrounds that included the now defunct NASCAR track, and there was a certain amount of nostalgia in the community about selling that particular piece of property. If we could bag up dirt from the track, we could market it as buying a piece of the fairgrounds. One of my staff members had a bunch of small linen bags he was willing to donate to

the cause, so we printed stickers of the fair's logo and stuck them onto the bags. Then we collected the dirt but decided we really should sterilize it so there wouldn't be any bugs or bacteria in it. We filled dishes with the red clay and put the dishes in the microwave for five minutes until the dirt was steaming. Then we proceeded to fill the bags. The hot dirt smelled like . . . dirt. It was also dry and powdery and got into our noses and eyes. We sneezed and hacked our way through several hours of dirt bagging, and when we were done, we had about two hundred bags of primo dirt that we planned to sell for five dollars each. Everyone on my Christmas list that year got a bag of fair dirt. I think we sold an additional twenty of them. I eventually threw out the rest. Ten years later, I still have my bag of dirt.

Our membership drive was board-inspired, so I take no responsibility for its failure. The first thing the board did was change the bylaws to allow non-voting associate memberships and gift memberships. Then they established membership levels that started at $25 and went up to $1,000. Two board members and I came in at the $250 benefactor level. Nearly everyone else stayed at the $25 individual member level. That year and in subsequent years until I retired, everyone on my Christmas list got a gift membership to the Fair Association, whether they wanted it or not. At least they liked the memberships better than the dirt bags.

Not all of my ideas were bad—really! The World's Greatest Garage Sale was a winner. We sold table space for $10 a table and charged people $1 a person to shop. People sold everything from real garage sale "treasures" to antiques to just plain junk. After the first sale, we had a waiting list of vendors and lines out the door of customers. If we timed the sales to coincide with a show in another building, our customers tripled. We began to do the garage sales whenever we had an open date in one of the buildings, and they always did very well. Yay for me!

Selling pull-tabs was another lucrative activity. Pull-tabs are like scratch-off lottery tickets except you pull off tabs instead of scratching off . . . well, you get the idea. The tickets were controlled by the New York State Gaming Commission, and we had to have a special license to sell them. We could make a maximum of $300 a box (a box normally had 1,000 tickets), so we had to sell a lot of boxes in order to make significant money. We always did well during the fair, especially in the Beer Tent and in the grandstand. The more people drank, the more tickets they bought. And there was an advantage to the chronically late-starting demolition derbies. People were bored so they bought tickets.

Selling pull-tabs at concerts also worked well. At the outdoor Bush concert, I was sitting at a table selling them when we were deluged by a pop-up shower. The boxes of pull-tabs weighed about ten pounds each and I had four of them. I couldn't leave them unattended because every box represented $300, but they were too heavy and bulky for me to carry, so I stashed them under the table, pushing aside several people who had taken shelter there. Then, like an idiot, I sat in the rain guarding them. I had a lawn chair with a collapsible roof that could be pulled up to ward off sun or rain. It was supposedly waterproof. It wasn't. My staff had all run for cover as soon as the first raindrops fell. They said they had briefly thought about rescuing me but had decided against it because it was raining too hard. I take back everything I previously said about having a great staff.

Like most communities, Monroe County had a "bed tax" that was paid by people renting hotel/motel rooms. The tax revenue was split among those venues that were instrumental in bringing tourism dollars to the region, including the Convention Center that got 25%, the downtown Blue Cross Arena that got 23.5%, the Visitors Association that got 50%, and the Fair Association that got 1.5%. The fact that two-thirds of all the hotel rooms in the county were in Henrietta didn't seem to make a difference to the allocation calculation. We also brought in at least twelve million in tourism dollars, so we felt the allocation was vastly unfair. We didn't want 25% of the allotment; an additional 1% (about $50,000) would have made a huge difference to our bottom line.

The board and I went on a campaign. "We're not asking for a hand-out," we said. "We just want our *fair* share." We wrote letters. We sent legislative members newspaper articles that showed all we were doing at the Fair and Expo Center to counteract the false claim that we were under-used. Several of my board members and I met individually with legislators on both sides of the aisle. We lobbied and spoke at legislative meetings. We even met with the county executive to plead our case. The result was that the legislature met and revised the allocation agreement. The decision was that the Fair Association's allocation would be *reduced* from 1.5% to 1%. I refer you to Chapter Seventeen: "I'm from the State Office and I'm Here to Help."

Most people thought that attending the fair was too expensive, but it cost about $225,000 to put on the event. Money had to come from somewhere. Sponsorships were hard to get because sponsors always wanted the biggest bang for their bucks. With the Erie County Fair and the New York State Fair in a sixty-mile radius from us, most sponsorship dollars went to either or both of them, leaving scant pickings for us. In reality, a fair was a bargain for consumers. Kids got into the fair for free, so with adult admission at $5 a person, for $10, a family of four could enjoy all the free entertainment and exhibits at the fair, far less than an afternoon at a movie theater. Too bad the public didn't see it that way. Of course, if you didn't bring a picnic lunch and had to add the cost of food, and the fees for carnival rides and grandstand events, it could get pricey.

To offset what was perceived by our community as a high cost for entertainment, our carnival company urged us to adopt a pay-one-price policy. The consumer would pay only once. His ticket would include gate admission, unlimited rides, all entertainment and exhibits, and grandstand events. In order for this pricing to work, *everyone* had to pay it. This system had worked well all over the country, resulting in increased attendance at pay-one-price fairs and subsequently, increased revenue for both the fairs and the carnivals. We decided to try it. We got more complaints in the three years of our pay-one-price fair than I got in the other seventeen years put together. People preferred to pay only for what they wanted and balked at "subsidizing" anyone else's entertainment. Senior citizens were especially adamant. They actually accosted me, yelling into my face about being ripped off. By the end of the fairs, I felt beaten up. And instead of going up, after the first year, our attendance actually went down. Again, what worked in other places simply did not work in Monroe County. Three years later, we abandoned the pay-one-price system and went back to pay-as-you-go. Even then, people never stopped complaining, arguing that fair admission should be free. I could never figure out the economics of that.

Each county fair in the country gets money from their states for premiums. Premiums are prize money that is paid to exhibitors for entering their livestock or other items into fairs. In New York, this money is spelled out in the Department of Agriculture and Markets law and has been on the books since the 1800s, but in 2001, there was opposition to this allocation on the part of some legislators, and premium money to fairs was threatened. If the money were taken from fairs, it would be very detrimental because most fairs always struggle financially. It would also deter exhibitors from entering into the fair's competitions, which is one of the traditional elements of all fairs. The New York State Association of Agricultural Fairs, along with several carnival companies who were active in New York State, decided to organize a lobby day where representatives from fairs and carnivals would go to the state capital, Albany, and speak with legislators. I decided I would be part of this delegation, which proved to be successful. We maintained our premium money, at least for one year.

The following year, I once again went to Albany for Lobby Day. The weather was dreadful: rainy, windy, and icy, which is typical for early March in New York State. Since my husband and I had been visiting our daughter in Albany, my husband dropped me off at the entrance to the Legislative Office Building, the same entrance I had used the previous year, and drove off to do some shopping while I lobbied. Braving the wind and rain, and juggling umbrella, briefcase, and purse, I battled up the steep and numerous steps to the front door of the building. A sign read: NO ENTRANCE. USE WASHINGTON STREET.

Being unfamiliar with Albany, I didn't know what street I was on, much less where Washington Street was, but I reasoned that if I walked around the building, I would eventually find the Washington Street entrance. What I didn't count on was that each side of the building was the length of a city block. As I walked, the icy rain started coming down heavily, and the wind whipped around the corners of the building, turning my umbrella inside out so that I was actually collecting rain rather than blocking it. Since I hadn't planned on walking outside, I had left my winter boots in my husband's car. I sloshed through ankle deep, slushy puddles while dodging icy patches on the sidewalk. I negotiated the entire building without finding that magic open door. I also never saw another living soul, and I was afraid I would slip on the ice and die of exposure before anyone found me. Finally, ignoring a sign that warned me not to, I pulled open a door and was immediately assaulted by the wail of sirens. Two very angry, uniformed police officers appeared at the door, and my life flashed before my eyes as I pictured being carried off to Guantanamo by Homeland Security—a frozen, wet, terrorist fair manager. The rest of the day was a blur, literally, because I lost one contact lens somewhere along the line, and spent the day squinting like a pirate. (By the way, the entrance was in a building across the street from the Legislative Office Building. It was a new, post-9/11 security entrance, complete with metal detectors, and it was connected to the office building by a tunnel under the road.) That was my final year of participating in Lobby Day.

CHAPTER TWENTY-ONE

It's at the Fairgrounds,
So it Must Be Free!

The fairgrounds were fairly isolated. The main buildings were a quarter of a mile from the roadway, and although there were a few light poles, the area was somewhat dark. We didn't have twenty-four hour security, so there was usually no one around from 5 p.m. to 8 a.m. That was a prime time for picking things up. Still, daylight didn't seem to deter some bold thieves.

One year on the day after the fair, we were in the process of putting things away. We had gotten a donation of some gardening tools and hoses, which we badly needed. My maintenance crew left them outside the back door of the Dome while they put away the forklift. When they returned a few minutes later, everything was gone. We checked the security tape and saw that a red pickup truck had pulled up to the door. A man got out of the truck, loaded the bed with the hoses and tools, and drove away. The security tape was too fuzzy to get a license plate number or a good look at the man, but we did see that there was a significant dent in the right rear fender of the truck. The next afternoon, the same thing happened with the disappearance of more portable equipment: same red truck, same man.

Now I was mad, so we tried setting a trap. We left stuff out and hid, hoping to catch the perpetrator in the act, but the man never returned. For months, I scrutinized and followed every red pickup truck I saw, looking for a dented right rear fender. I'm not sure what I planned to do if I actually found it, but I was definitely on a mission.

During one fair, we did a hydroponics display in Spaceport and borrowed several grow lights from Cornell University. The plants were doing fine until one morning, we noticed that it looked suspiciously dark where the plants were situated. Sometime during the night, all the lights had disappeared. Apparently, those kinds of lights are great for growing marijuana, and they cost about $200 each. We never saw them again, and all our plants died.

Lights seemed to be at a premium that year. We rented a number of security lights, the kind you see along the highway during night construction work, to provide illumination in areas of the fair that we felt were unsafe. The night after the fair was over, someone stole all of those security lights as well. It must have been quite the marijuana growing operation.

Golf carts were like beacons of light to thieves. We rented the carts from a local company, and since they were in high demand for summer festivals, the rental company always picked them up the night the fair closed. One year, the dispatcher called and said that the carts would not be picked up until the following morning. My secretary, who didn't realize that they would be left outside with the keys in them, neglected to inform maintenance of the new schedule. The next morning, the rental company came to pick up the carts, and they were nowhere in sight. My crew eventually found them in the meadow, totally smashed as a result of some kids who had decided to stage their own demolition derby.

But the theft that most amazed me happened while I was in North Carolina, working with the carnival. I was sitting in the airport in Charlotte, waiting for my connecting flight home, when my events director called on my cell phone. She said that our ATM had been stolen from the lobby. The machine was bolted to the floor, and yet someone had backed up to the glass door, broken the glass, and carried the whole thing away, money and all. By the time the police responded to the alarm, the perpetrators were long gone and so was the ATM. It was a new machine that had recently been installed. An investigation of the discarded bolts showed that they had not been tightened, making it a snap to remove the ATM from the concrete floor. The insurance company decided it was the fault of the installers and probably an inside job.

We went through one really bad period where little things went missing. This happened just before the fair when I was purchasing small prizes for various contests as well as organizing place ribbons and rosettes that would be awarded for winners in certain classes. I had one rosette labeled "Best Cock." This was for the best male chicken in the poultry show. That rosette always made me giggle. Apparently someone else thought it was funny too, because it disappeared. I still wonder who got that rosette and what was used as criteria for the decision to award it.

We used hundreds of hay bales as buffers in the track area where we had the sprint car races. Since each bale cost us $2, after one fair, my crew piled the hay along the periphery of the track where we planned to store it for the winter and re-use it at the next fair. However, I got a call from the dispatcher at the Henrietta Fire Department telling me there was a fire on the track and that I needed to meet the fire chief there. I had just gone to sleep when I got the call, so I got dressed and drove the eight miles to the fairgrounds, grousing and fretting for the entire drive. I figured it was just a small fire that would be out by the time I got there, but as I drew closer, all I could see was red sky and black smoke.

Without lights, the track area was very secluded, and some kids apparently decided it was a great place to have a bonfire. The dry hay was the perfect fodder, and the fire was soon out of control. Since there was no water source at the track, the firefighters had to pump water from the retention pond in order to douse the flames, a much trickier operation than simply attaching a hose to a hydrant. By the next morning, the fire was still smoldering.

All the buildings on the fairgrounds were alarmed, which was somewhat of a deterrent to theft. It was up to the last person out of the facility to set the alarm. Maintenance was supposed to make certain that the doors in the connecting buildings were closed and latched before they left for the day so that the alarm would set. As I was most often the last one to leave, it usually fell to me to alarm the buildings.

Many times, this was impossible because one or more of the doors was not closed all the way. Then I needed to venture into the Dome to find which of them was not secure.

It was spooky being in such a large building alone, and I hated leaving my office and going into the arena, especially at night when it was lit only by meager emergency lighting. It was dark and shadowy, and there were too many hiding places and too many dark corners, even though the building was round. Also, my maintenance crew swore the Dome was haunted. They said they would sometimes leave equipment in one location and return to find it in an entirely different place. I could never shake the feeling that someone was watching me when I wandered into the Dome alone at night, and I always hurried, constantly looking over my shoulder as I checked all the doors.

Fittingly, the alarm system was just as finicky as every other piece of equipment at the fairgrounds. There was one motion sensor in the boiler room that seemed to be triggered by nothing in particular or everything in general. More times than I can count, I got a call at night from the security monitoring company, asking me to meet a sheriff's deputy so we could check out an alarm. This usually happened sometime between 1 a.m. and 3 a.m. when I was in a sound sleep. Cold winter nights were the worst. The culprit was almost always the sensor in the boiler room. (When I first came to the executive director's position and before we installed a new security system that had a silent alarm, anytime there was a security breach, a loud and annoying claxon would sound outside, waking the entire community in near proximity to the fairgrounds. It's no wonder the neighbors hated us.)

Despite the fact that the calls were usually false alarms, working with the police was invariably professional and polite, and they always kept me protected as we did our searches of the premises. In my twenty years at the Dome, we never found an intruder—although, on several occasions, we did find people doing donuts or having romantic trysts in the parking lot.

A Family, A' Fair

Most people who get involved with fairs do so because they have a family history with them. Either they grew up on a farm, or were 4-H members as kids, or their families always participated in fairs. I was the exception since I came to fairs long after I was an adult. Still, in many fairs throughout the country, it's not unusual to find multiple family members on the board of directors or as department superintendents.

When I first came to the Monroe County Fair, although there were some people on the board who had a past connection to the fair, they didn't seem to have any loyalty or desire to participate in it. Even one of our most influential board members, who sold agricultural equipment, urged us to disband the fair and to simply give out scholarships to kids who planned on going into the agricultural field. He believed that fairs were things of the past. Since I was a true believer in the value of fairs, I knew that I needed to change the culture of the board and of the fair if it were going to survive.

Over the years, the board gradually changed. I found past 4-H members who agreed to be on the board or to be department heads. With them came their children who also participated and who gradually took on leadership roles. My own family was no exception.

With the hours I worked, if my family wanted to see me at all, they needed to become involved with the fair. All of them did in one form or another.

As I mentioned before, my oldest daughter was my secretary/ receptionist for about nine months. We even got her future husband involved. He was a landscape architect, and he built a beautiful stone planter that surrounded our marquee sign.

My middle child had taken dancing lessons for most of her life, and she and her husband competed in ballroom dancing competitions, so they were both naturals to judge our talent shows. Because my daughter had a career in marketing, she often helped with our public relations and promotional efforts as well. Since she was germ phobic, she tended to stay away from the more agricultural areas of the fair.

But it was my youngest child, Michael, who really embraced the fair. He was twelve years old when I started working at the fairgrounds, and he always wanted to help me. His first job was picking up rocks that seemed to be asexually multiplying. Even that horrible job didn't deter him, and he often asked if he could have my job when I was ready to retire. He thought it would be great fun to be the boss and to fire people. (It's not!)

As he got older, he became our summer intern. I recently asked him what his job was as an intern, and he said, "Lackey." He was right. The intern got all the jobs no one else wanted. But Michael was the type of guy who got along with everyone, from board members to the maintenance crew, and everyone liked him. He never pulled the "I'm the son of the executive director" card. If there was a job to be done, no matter how dirty or sweaty, Michael pitched in because he loved the fair and wanted to see it succeed.

Michael's biggest job was that of concessions manager. He needed to book food and merchandise vendors for the outside areas of the fair, help them to get situated when they arrived, and keep them happy during the duration of the fair, the latter being an impossibility. Vendors notoriously complained about everything, and Michael tended to hide from them whenever possible.

He was also in charge of the talent show as well as the other entertainers in our Festival Tent (which he found was a good place to hide from the complaining vendors.) His job was to make sure that the sound technicians had everything they needed and that the bands had all the perks that were specified in their contracts, like beer, food, and water. Some bands wanted specific brands of beer, elaborate meals, or designer waters, but we usually nixed those. We didn't have money for frills, so they got whatever water was cheapest and whatever beer brand sponsored the fair for that year. If they had to have food, Michael would cajole a food vendor into donating it.

Michael's other job, especially before the fair, was as a gofer. We sent him all over the county to pick up things, from cheese samples for the Ag Ed Center to trophies for livestock shows. Once we sent him to a 4-H leader's house to pick up a spinning wheel that would be used by a demonstrator in the Home Arts Department. The 4-H leader had just made zucchini soup, so she insisted that Michael stay for lunch. My vegetable-phobic son dutifully ate the soup but afterward insisted he wanted hazardous duty pay.

Since we always required many cases of water during the fair for staff consumption, entertainers, and our own concession stand, one year we sent Michael to Sam's Club to pick up numerous cases. He decided that he wanted to get all the cases back to the fairgrounds without having to travel more than once over the vast distance (of one mile) to and from Sam's Club. So he tied all the cases to the top of our old maintenance truck. Everything was fine until he made the turn into the fair's parking lot. That's when the whole load shifted. We watched from the window in my office as the cases seemed to fall off the truck's roof in slow motion. We salvaged what we could, washing mud off the bottles that didn't break (while I fretted about E. coli contamination from the dirt.) The worst part (for Michael) was that his future wife, Laura, who now worked at the fair and shared the summer intern job with him, had warned him not to put that many cases on top of the truck. After fifteen years of marriage, he is still trying to live that one down.

Laura started working at the fair when she and Michael were dating. They actually met at the fairgrounds when we hosted a 4-H teen lock-in when they were both teenagers. Laura fit right in and came to love the fair as much as Michael did. Even after her first child was born, she got a babysitter so she could help out in the office during the fair. Laura was our resident meteorologist. She had a knack for figuring out weather patterns, and I called her multiple times a day as I obsessed about our western sky, wondering if the ominous clouds would pass us or become major headaches. Her assessments were usually right.

My husband also "worked" for the fair. His self-proclaimed "job" was as food tester. He would eat at all the concession stands and then report back as to which ones had the tastiest offerings. Since I was usually too nervous to eat during the fair, I had to take his word for it. He maintained that he had the best job of us all, and I do believe that was true.

CHAPTER TWENTY-THREE

Hail to Me (the Chief)

I had been Executive Director of the Monroe County Fair Association for several years when I decided that I wanted to get active in the New York State Association of Agricultural Fairs. I submitted my résumé to the nominating committee and was elected to go through the chairs, serving as president in 2000, only the third woman to be elected president in the 112 years of the association's existence. Even though the convention where I was nominated was held in Rochester, my fair's home city, no member of my board was at the convention that day to support me. That made me very sad and was a telling reminder that I needed to change the culture of our association.

I loved being president, and when my term ended, I hated to relinquish it. I wanted to name myself Czarina or Empress, similar to what Napoleon had done, and to remain in office, lapping up all the prestige and glamour.

As president, I presided over the annual convention, which that year happened to coincide with my birthday. Since I had been instrumental in moving the convention to Rochester from Syracuse, a real coup for the Rochester Visitors Association, the hotel staff and the Visitors Association determined that they would do something nice for me as a thank you/birthday present. They decided that on the day of my birthday, they would move me from my standard hotel room to their prime suite.

The suite was beautiful. It was on the top floor of the Hyatt and had a panoramic view of the city. The living room was so large that it even held a grand piano. I couldn't really see what the bedroom was like as, by the time I got there, my husband had been asleep for several hours, so I didn't turn on the light. I was so busy with convention duties that I didn't get to my room until midnight. Since I needed to preside at a 9 a.m. meeting, I spent a total of nine hours in the suite and was asleep for eight of those hours. Because the hotel staff had actually moved my belongings, I had no idea where they put anything, so getting dressed in the morning was a treasure hunt. But my husband, who ordered room service and spent the evening in the room while I was working, really enjoyed it. I wish I had.

And while I'm on the topic of conventions, for many, many years, the New York State Association of Agricultural Fairs Convention had been held in Syracuse at the historic Hotel Syracuse. The hotel had a spectacular lobby that became a communal meeting space. It sported a wall-length bar on one side of a softly lit, huge, carpeted room. Cozy, comfortable sofas and chairs were strategically placed in a random array that invited people to linger and to socialize. Carnivals, fairs, concessionaires, entertainers, and vendors all gathered in various parts of the room for informal chats or for more formal contract signing meetings.

The hotel also had one of the most beautiful ballrooms I have ever seen. The room was decorated in white with gilt highlights and trim that glittered from the crystals of a magnificent chandelier. A pillared balcony surrounded the lushly carpeted room, and from that perch you could almost see and hear the music and dancing from long ago cotillions. The rest of the hotel was a dump.

In 1993 on a cold, snowy, January day, I went to that hotel—my first convention as fair manager. I checked in and got the key to my room. It was a big, ornately decorated, metal key that fit into the sizable lock of a darkly stained, solid oak door that was reminiscent of bygone days of opulence. I opened the door, expecting the opulence to continue, and instead found a small, dimly lit room that held a bed and a nightstand. Period. There was barely room enough to move around the bed to get to the bathroom.

The bathroom was the size of a closet into which a trestle sink, a toilet, and a small shower stall had been crammed. The shower itself had no door or curtain. There were also no curtains, blinds, or shades on the bathroom window, which faced other rooms in the hotel, and there was no door on the bathroom. Unless I wanted to provide a peep show for other hotel guests, I needed to crawl from the shower to the bedroom in order to get dressed. The good news was that I did have heat in my room, but other rooms had either heat that couldn't be turned off or no heat at all, and you never knew which room you were likely to get. The same held true for meeting rooms. You either froze or sweltered, sometimes switching modes several times in a day. Finally the decision was made to move the convention to a more stable environment. Hence the move to Rochester.

One of the highlights of every convention was the showmen's party that our carnival company organized. It was always a costume party, and there was usually a DJ. The first year that I was fair manager, the theme was Pirates and Wenches, and I found the perfect pirate costume that was kind of sexy yet tasteful. (My husband nixed the sexy part, saying something like, "You are going to put something on under that top. Right?) I figured no one knew who I was as yet, since I had only been fair manager for a few months, so I could really let loose. I danced with abandon. I drank—a lot. Unfortunately, they did know who I was, and I never lived it down. I showed much more decorum in subsequent years, but I have to admit that I had the best time of my life at that first party.

But back to my year as president. One of the things I did that summer was go to as many fairs as possible. In two months, I put 5,000 miles on my car and visited thirty-two of the forty-nine fairs in the state. I probably could have traveled fewer miles, but, like my father, I must have been born without the gene that allows people to instinctively know which way is north, south, east, or west. Discerning left from right was marginally better. I had a 50/50 chance of getting it right. GPS was fairly new in 2000, so all I had was a road map, and my map reading skills were only a trifle better than my directional skills.

The fair I had the most trouble finding was the one in Altamont, New York. Altamont is a very small town that is a little east, west, north, or south of Albany. I couldn't find it on the map, so I winged it. I passed the same gas station three times, sort of like *National Lampoon's European Vacation* ("Look, kids. Big Ben. Parliament.") before I stopped for directions.

Although all the fairs I visited were in New York State, each fair varied from its counterparts in so many ways. The state was home to one of the largest fairs in the United States but also home to one of the smallest. Each week of my travels was a different experience.

The Erie County Fair ("America's Fair") was the third largest fair in the country. Because of its location, it drew attendance and exhibitors from Western New York as well as from Ohio, Canada, and Pennsylvania. Its carnival was huge with sixty or more rides, it had more entertainment venues than we had at five fairs combined, and it would take a month to eat at all the food stands. This fair not only had a harness racing track, but in 2004, New York State allowed the track to add video lottery terminals (also known as slot machines) as well. This was a huge financial boon to the fair that allowed it to grow into the behemoth it is now.

The year I was president, we had a fair manager's meeting in the clubhouse of the Erie County Fair's racetrack, and after dinner, I was asked to ride in the pace car for one of the harness races. (This was a normal pace car that didn't involve fire suits, straps, or helmets.) Riding in that pace car was one of the most thrilling things I have ever done. We rode in front of six horses that were attached to sulkies. The car gradually picked up speed until the horses were on pace, and then we peeled off to the side while the horses raced past us. As we sped down the straightaway, I looked behind me. I will never forget the fierce look on the jockeys' faces nor the thundering hooves of the horses. After the race, I got to put the blanket on the winning horse.

The Yates County Fair was probably the smallest fair in the state. I especially liked it for its homemade pie booth. The rhubarb pie was my favorite, mainly because no one else in my family would ever eat it, so I rarely got to have that particular treat.

And speaking of pies, the Wayne County Fair, which was just over the county line from us, had a very successful annual pie auction that earned a goodly amount of money for them. People got to know who made the best pies, and the auction was always a lively highlight of the fair. Unfortunately, the Health Department rules in Monroe County would not allow any foods to be consumed or purchased at our fair unless they had been prepared in county certified kitchens. That took away a lot of the "flavor" that county fairs had always enjoyed.

That brings to mind an experience I had with a certified kitchen when I was the 4-H liaison to the fair's board of directors and before I became executive director. My 4-H rabbit club needed to earn some money, so somebody (I swear it wasn't me) decided we should make pies to sell at the fair. I booked the kitchen at the county certified facility at Cooperative Extension, and one Saturday morning, my forty 4-H club members gathered to make pies. Unfortunately, my co-leader had a family emergency, so I was on my own.

Trying to teach forty kids that pie dough should not be kneaded, as well as the logistics of getting the dough from the table to the pan, was hard enough. Keeping track of forty easily bored kids, whose ages ranged from seven to seventeen, was an impossible feat. By the time we were done, the kitchen was a disaster with bowls, measuring cups, and spoons in the sink, on tables, and on the floor, and a thin film of flour covered every flat surface of the kitchen and the adjoining meeting room. There were also flour footprints throughout the two floors of the building, the kids had flour in their hair as well as in their ears from "flour wars," and I was covered in flour, out of patience, and exhausted. Nevertheless, we had cherry and peach pies that were ready for the fair, and if they were not totally delicious, they were at least edible, and the public seemed eager to support the 4-H kids. We served the pies with what we euphemistically called "4-H lemonade." Because we were 4-H'ers, everyone assumed it was made from hand-squeezed lemons, but it was actually Country Time Lemonade Mix to which we had added cut pieces of lemon. We were usually silent when people told us how good it was.

But, more about my travels. My favorite fairgrounds were the Trumansburg fairgrounds in Tompkins County. It had trees. Our fair had two deciduous trees, one of which was cut down when the fairgrounds were renovated, so shade was always at a premium and usually achieved by erecting tents that shielded the sun but still held in the heat, essentially creating ovens. I envied fairgrounds that had shaded areas where their patrons could get respite from the summer heat instead of frying or turning into puddles of sweat as they did at our fair. I also envied Trumansburg for being able to draw attendance from summer school students at Cornell University and Ithaca College as well as from tourists to Watkins Glen and the Finger Lakes. Its attendance always surpassed ours despite Rochester being a bigger metropolitan area.

I was pretty good friends with the manager of the Delaware County Fair, which was in the southern tier of the state. It was in a rural area, and there was only one motel within easy driving distance. My friend kept asking me when I was coming to the fair because he wanted to make sure he reserved a room at the motel for me. He said it booked up quickly during fair week. So I picked a date, and he reserved a room. I spent the day at the fair, and its board threw out the red carpet for me. In the early evening, I got directions and headed to the motel.

The motel was an old-style construction—"old" being the key word here. It was a one-story building with connected rooms that faced the road. When I pulled into the graveled parking lot, there were several old pickup trucks, along with a number of men swilling beer, who were mostly located directly in front of the door to my room. The door itself was only about a half-inch thick with a lock on it that would switch from opened to closed if you hit the doorknob just right. When I entered the room, it was dark and dingy and smelled sour. I took one look and decided there was no way in hell I was staying in that room, especially by myself, so I went back to the office and told the attendant I had changed my mind and would not be staying after all. She said that my friend had already paid for the room. I didn't want to hurt his feelings or to appear snobbish, so I told the room clerk not to tell my friend that I wasn't staying. If she could re-let the room, she was free to do so. It would be our little secret. Then I left and drove to Oneonta where I stayed in a brand new hotel.

Several months later, I was at the New York State Fairs Convention when I ran into the people from Delaware County. They said they had been worried about me. When I looked puzzled, they told me that there had been a fire at the motel the night I was supposedly staying there. I said I had undoubtedly slept through the whole thing, which is technically true. I was sleeping soundly at the Holiday Inn Express in Oneonta.

Each year, passes are issued by the New York State Association of Agricultural Fairs that allow other fair managers, along with people who purchase them, to get into fairs across the state free of charge. Whoever is president of the association for that year signs the passes. Gate attendants at all the fairs are supposed to recognize the passes and allow the bearers to enter. That doesn't always work very well. At one fair, I simply was not going to be allowed entry. I explained that I was president of the association. I showed the guard my name on the pass as well as my driver's license that bore the same name. Nope. After about fifteen minutes, the guard finally contacted someone in the fair office who agreed to let me come in. If I had any illusions about my glamour and prestige, it evaporated in that fifteen minutes.

But I loved being president. Three times a year, I wrote an article for the Fair Association's newsletter, letting member fairs know what an honor it was to serve them. I did tell them that it wasn't all lollipops and roses, though, especially since the brouhaha over water testing happened during that year. At the final meeting of my tenure, the incoming president presented me with a bag of lollipops and a beautiful bouquet of roses. That sort of made up for not being made Empress.

Photo of me as president of the NYSAAF in 2000 when my theme for the convention was "The Fair—A Snapshot of America"

September 11, 2001

I was listening to the radio on my way to work when I heard about the first plane hitting the World Trade Center. At first, I thought it must have been pilot error. I remember looking at the sky. It was a beautifully clear day, and I expected that the weather in New York City would be similar to ours. I was puzzling over how a pilot could make such a significant miscalculation on a beautiful, clear day when the second plane hit. That's when I realized we were being attacked. I started to cry, not just for the victims, but also for what I knew would come next. I knew it was the beginning of the end of our freedoms. Many of the rights we took for granted would be lost in the name of security.

By the time I got to work, my staff already had the TV on in my office, and they were huddled around it. We had interviews scheduled that day for a vacant events director position, so we turned off the TV and tried to focus on the interviews. My bookkeeper, who had a radio in her office, came in several times to give us updates, including when the first tower collapsed. It was awful trying to conduct business as usual when nothing was usual.

As soon as I had an opportunity, I called our county legislator. Planes had just been grounded, and at that point, we had no information as to how many people would be stranded in Rochester because of the grounding. I offered the Dome as an emergency shelter for anyone who couldn't get home and who couldn't find a hotel room. As it turned out, the Dome wasn't needed for that purpose, but it was needed for a Red Cross blood drive. On September 14, we had hundreds of people show up to give blood. Some waited in line for hours. The donors were very subdued and somber. At noon, there was a nationwide moment of silence, followed by the playing of the National Anthem. There were lots of tears that day, along with dread. No one knew what would happen next.

With everyone thinking about emergency preparedness, during the succeeding months and for several years thereafter, the Dome was considered a viable location for a number of emergency situations. We worked with the Red Cross and became a designated evacuation center for that agency. We also became the emergency evacuation site for the Rush-Henrietta School District and the Rochester Psychiatric Hospital. The Monroe County Department of Health chose the facility for annual flu clinics, and in 2009 during the H1N1 (swine flu) epidemic, the Dome was selected as an inoculation site by the New York State Health Department. New York State and Monroe County officials developed detailed plans and conducted numerous drills so that vaccinations could be done quickly and efficiently. (In 2021, the Dome also became a designated New York State vaccination site during the COVID-19 pandemic.)

For several years before 2001, we had been hosting Islamic prayer services, one in the fall and one in the spring, to coincide with Muslim holidays. The fall service was only a month or two after 9/11, and I was very nervous about it. I wasn't worried about danger from the Islamic worshipers. I was worried because most of the Muslims in our community would be congregated in our facility, and I feared that someone might want to retaliate for 9/11 and set off a bomb.

I had numerous conversations with agents at the FBI who assured me that they had detected no chatter about possible retaliation. Nevertheless, I devised a new protocol for those events. We would not publicize the prayer service on our marquee sign, as we usually did. Additionally, no boxes or equipment were to be left outside around the perimeter of the Dome. If anything appeared, we would know it was not ours and therefore suspicious. The same went for any boxes or equipment inside the buildings. Packages left behind after the event were considered suspect as well. Also, interior doors were to be kept locked so we could monitor the movement of people, and staff were directed to walk around at all times, looking for anything that seemed out of the ordinary.

Fortunately, there were no problems, and we continued to enjoy a good relationship with the Islamic Center leaders for many years. Still, that first event post 9/11 was very stressful.

CHAPTER TWENTY-FIVE
On Being a Woman Executive
Before It was Fashionable

In recent years, there has been a lot of talk about sexual harassment and what constitutes it. I can honestly say that in my twenty years of working for the fair, there was only one time when I truly felt uncomfortable.

Each year, the International Association of Fairs and Expositions holds zone meetings in various parts of the country. One year, the zone meeting for our region was to be held in Vermont. I had two choices. I could drive myself to Vermont, but with my sense of direction, or lack thereof, the conference would be over before I ever found it. Or I could hitch a ride with other fair people from our zone. Since, at that time, there were few women fair managers, it was inevitable that I was going to be traveling with some of my male counterparts. I asked people from a fair located to the west of us if I could travel along with them. They had to pass through Rochester anyway, so it was an easy solution.

There were three men and me in the car for the six-hour drive. I didn't know any of the men very well. They were all in their late fifties or early sixties, so we are not talking teenagers. Despite that, throughout the six-hour drive, they acted like teenagers, farting and telling dirty, sexist jokes. Basically shy by nature, I didn't know how to react. Was I supposed to laugh at the jokes? Was I supposed to ignore the farts? It was truly an uncomfortable, and somewhat odoriferous, ride. On the way home, I sat in the back and pretended to sleep the whole way. That eliminated my having to react or interact.

Even though that was the only time I was uncomfortable, that doesn't mean I wasn't aware that I was being held to a different standard than a man would be in the position I held. For example, I was accused by several members of my board of being intimidating. I am five feet-two inches tall, so I'm not exactly physically imposing. But when I went into a board meeting, especially if we were going to be discussing something controversial, I always had a written agenda, my points were enumerated, and I was prepared to answer questions with facts and figures. If a man went into a meeting with this same *modus operandi*, he would be considered businesslike and professional. I, however, was considered intimidating.

When I first became executive director, there were a number of men on my board and in the community who weren't happy to have a woman at the helm. They were not only waiting for me to make a serious error, but they were also actively looking for ways to undermine me. I remember one meeting in particular. It was shortly after the resignation of the former executive director and the board president, and we were trying to find our way through some pretty intense problems, not the least of which was a public relations nightmare caused by the media insisting that something nefarious was going on. At the executive committee meeting, one of the older male board members kept challenging everything I said. Finally, I slapped my hand on the table and turned to him.

"Look. I am doing the best I can under very difficult circumstances. You can either be part of the solution or part of the problem."

His response? "Well, isn't that ladylike!"

I wasn't trying to be ladylike or man-like. I was just trying to do the job, but that, apparently, was very threatening.

Although this type of negativity improved through the years, I was always aware that I could not afford to make a mistake. This put a lot of pressure on me to perform. Every executive knows that the secret to being a good leader is to be surrounded by people who have strengths to buttress your weaknesses. No one person can be an expert in everything. But certain members of my board expected me to be proficient in everything from plumbing to oratory, and they were quick to point out my deficiencies, even when everything was running smoothly.

Although I never hid anything from board members, I always made certain that I had solutions to problems before I presented the problems. With this wariness on my part, I perceived my board to be more adversaries than partners, something that was detrimental not only to my peace of mind, but also to the success of our prime mission: the fair.

One of the things that drove me crazy was the unwillingness of certain board members to accept that I knew what I was doing. Many times, I was forced into paying big bucks to a consultant who eventually came to the same conclusions that I had come to months earlier. I always suspected that my credibility was questioned because of my gender.

I felt the glass ceiling when I applied for a board position on the International Association of Fairs and Expositions, a wonderful organization that provides networking experiences for small, medium, and large fairs through conferences and newsletters. Each year, there is a convention where fairs can share ideas and problems and learn trends in the industry. I never came away from those conventions without several new ideas that I wanted to implement at our fair.

But the association had a flaw. Although more than fifty percent of the membership was comprised of small fairs, most of the board members were from large fairs or state fairs. The voice of the small fair, I felt, was missing, so I decided to try for a board position.

I am not a schmoozer. I don't play golf or tennis. I don't sit at a bar and make small talk with other people in the industry. It's just not in my nature to do this. That doesn't make me less competent or less social. But I'm just not a "good ole boy," and that's what I needed to be to get the job on the board. I am happy to say that things have changed since that time. Now half of the board of directors are women, as are half of the members of the executive committee. In fact, the newest executive director is a woman. (Moreover, since 2015, there has been at least one zone director each year who is from a small fair.) I call that progress, but at the time I was applying for a board position, it sure was difficult for a woman to break that barrier.

I guess I believed in women's lib before it became popular. I grew up with sisters. My father, although very traditional and conservative, strongly believed in education for women at a time when that opinion was not very common. Even members of my extended family questioned why I wanted to go to college when I was "just going to get married anyway." But I was a good student, and my father bucked family tradition and encouraged me to pursue my education. When he died, I had two choices: I could wallow in self-pity and screw up my life, or I could try to achieve the goals that he and I had shared. I felt that what I made of myself depended on me and nobody else. Until college, I never even considered that I couldn't do anything I wanted because of my gender. It was a pretty hard lesson when I was confronted by people who were not only intimidated by my abilities, but who also actively disliked me for having them.

Still, while I was living it, the gender bias I encountered seemed normal, and I just ignored it and tried to do my job. Only in retrospect did I realize how awful it was and how much smoother things would have gone if I had had a little cooperation. Instead, I constantly needed to prove myself and to stay one step ahead of the detractors who couldn't seem to adjust to having a woman in charge. I had to be very strong, very organized, and never acknowledge how their sexism affected me. That's pretty sad.

CHAPTER TWENTY-SIX
All You Need to Know
Happens in Vegas

Each year, the International Association of Fairs and Expositions held a convention in Las Vegas. To my board's credit, they never gave me any problem about attending this conference, despite its location. In fact, several times, board members accompanied me on the trip.

I'll never forget the first time I went to Las Vegas for this convention. I was walking (floating) down The Strip one night, admiring all the lights and the exciting ambiance. I couldn't believe that I was actually there! During the days, I dutifully attended every session and workshop, and in the evenings, I learned how to play video poker and found that I very much loved the taste of mudslides.

Over 5,000 delegates typically attended that convention, and they came from fairs all over the country as well as from Canada, Mexico, and Australia. They came from privately owned fairs like ours and from fairs owned by their counties or states. I found that large, medium, and small fairs, even gigantic state fairs, all shared the same joys, problems, concerns, successes, and failures. Actually, the only difference between small fairs and large fairs is that large fairs have more extravagant budgets, but they still have to make them balance just as every other fair does.

Most people don't realize that their county fair is not just an isolated community festival. It is actually part of a network of 2,000 fairs in North America who all share the same goals: to showcase their communities and to support and promote agriculture. At the conferences, fair managers and boards talk about how they can best do those things and how they can create great experiences that will be both fun and educational.

Sharing ideas was a great benefit of the convention. Even ideas from a large fair could be scaled back to work at a small one. Sometimes, a germ of an idea took root because of something someone said or did, and it was fun to see what new concepts took shape after attending a session. For example, after hearing about something similar that had been done at a state fair, we designed a toddler play area that included a room for nursing mothers.

Fairs are designed to be fun, but there are many serious issues that fair managers must address in order to keep them that way. Safety and health regulations top the list, and there were always seminars on E. coli infections, avian influenza, and other diseases that might affect livestock herds or fair attendees. Ride safety, gang violence, insurance needs, storm protocols, water quality issues, marketing, finance, human resources, foundations, and volunteer recruiting and retention were also topics that were discussed on a regular basis.

In the trade show, fairs looked for new and innovative entertainers, cutting-edge products that would make fairs easier to produce, and the latest trends in fair foods. At one convention, I found a company that made plastic tablecloths that had elasticized ends. Before I purchased these, my staff would spend hours cutting rolls of plastic to fit the hundreds of tables we used at the fair and then taping the ends of the plastic to the bottom of each table so the wind wouldn't blow away the coverings. The tape usually didn't hold, so we were constantly redoing our work. These new tablecloths saved us time and frustration and kept the senior citizen bingo players from complaining about table splinters. Also, the first time I saw Dippin' Dots ice cream was at the Las Vegas trade show, and I sampled chocolate Merlot ice cream when it was introduced at one of the zone meetings, finding it funny that I needed to show ID before I was served.

One year, I was asked to teach a workshop about inexpensive ways to promote and advertise a fair. I was pretty much an expert on that topic since I was never able to increase my advertising budget despite the fact that advertising costs had at least doubled in my twenty years as executive director. Nevertheless, I was pretty nervous about presenting before such an auspicious audience. I talked about how to write press releases, something few people knew how to do well, and how to pester editors until they were published. I encouraged people to send letters and essays to the Op Ed pages of their local newspapers, and how to write public service announcements that would meet the guidelines of most radio and TV stations. Mascots and parades were another cheap and effective form of advertising that could be used in multiple ways. I also talked about our outreach with community service projects and the teaching programs that we did with Cooperative Extension. After the session, someone from one of the larger fairs said he had gotten a lot of good ideas from my workshop. Did that make me feel good!

The work at the convention was fun because, for four days, I got to talk non-stop with people who shared my enthusiasm for fairs. But besides the work, there were other fun aspects to the trip.

Our carnival owner always took all his fair managers and boards out for a lavish dinner at a fabulous Las Vegas restaurant. There were probably eighty to a hundred people at those dinners that included an open bar, appetizers, a full course meal, and dessert. At Las Vegas prices, I would not have wanted to be the one footing the bill.

I always tried to attend at least one show while I was in Las Vegas. I saw Johnny Mathias, Barry Manilow, Anne Murray, Wayne Newton, the Rat Pack, Lance Burton, Charro, and of course, no Las Vegas trip would be complete without seeing the burlesque show at the Hilton. One year, a board member, who tended to be slightly on the naïve side, accompanied me to that show. She began feeling uncomfortable and very sorry for a show girl who she thought had had a wardrobe malfunction—until she realized that most of the other girls in the show were completely topless.

Although I loved playing slot machines, I was never very lucky. My friends from the Delaware County Fair always seemed to win. I thought if I went with them, some of their luck would rub off on me, but apparently, it doesn't work that way. However, once I actually won

$2,500 on a slot machine. I was with some friends from the carnival, and I stopped to put $1 into a haywire machine. That is a machine that will stop and then spin a few extra times for some unknown reason that I will never understand. I had not encountered that kind of machine before, so I thought it was broken. When the bells started ringing, indicating that I was a winner, I thought for sure I would be arrested for tampering with the machine. I couldn't believe it when the attendant actually handed me twenty-five, one-hundred-dollar bills! That money came at a very opportune time, however. When I got home from Las Vegas, my new puppy (that my son was supposed to be watching) had gotten out of his cage and had chewed up all the upholstered furniture in the living room. The tab to replace everything was just over $2,500.

I did win one other thing. At the trade show drawing during one convention, I won a ten-piece set of waterless cookware, probably the same kind of cookware I had registered to win at the Santa Maria fair some thirty years before. After being married for forty years, I was still using the same old CorningWare I had gotten as a wedding present. I smile a little every time I use the new set.

My Love/Hate Relationship
with the Town

In 1992 after the first few months of my tenure as executive director, we got an offer from a real estate development company that wanted to land-lease the meadow. The project it presented included an indoor soccer arena as well as a number of outdoor soccer fields. At the time, we were not using that portion of the land, and the idea seemed wonderful. We could support youth—one of the prime missions of the Fair Association—have a soccer tournament as part of the fair, and gain some much needed income on a year-round basis.

As with all construction projects, the potential buyer had many hoops to jump through before the town would give its approval to proceed. The first such hoop was presenting the plan to an open session of the town board. Word about the potential building of this complex spread rapidly throughout the town, and there was a lot of buzz about the upcoming town board meeting. I needed to be part of this discussion to validate that the Fair Association was in favor of the project, so I innocently went to the meeting.

I was living in California when the Dome and Minett Hall were built, so I had no knowledge of the terrible ill will the town's population harbored for the Fair Association as a result of the "never used ice arena" debacle. As I was sitting in the audience at the town board meeting, neighbor after neighbor got up to talk, blasting the Fair Association for "taking away their ice," and questioning why they should trust that this new complex would actually come to fruition and benefit them. I was stunned and wondered what the heck I had walked into when I took the job with the Fair Association. I was advocating for something good that would benefit the town's youth, and I was immediately suspected of being a charlatan and of working for an organization that was less than honorable.

When I got back to my office, I did some research so I could at least respond to allegations of fraud with some degree of intelligence. As I understand it, in the early 1970s, Barton Baker (an attorney and educator) left money to the Fair Association for the purpose of building a youth education center. There was a stipulation that his estate would donate half the money if the Fair Association would raise the other half of the needed funds. A capital campaign ensued, and the people of Henrietta donated money for this purpose. It wasn't nearly enough, so the Fair Association eventually got a loan (called a lease) from the Empire State Development Corporation, and they proceeded to build the Dome and Minett Hall as ice arenas. (As an interesting side note, Minett Hall bears the name of the attorney who brokered the deal rather than the philanthropist who actually donated the money.)

As luck would have it, the buildings were completed in 1973, just when the energy crunch hit, so it was financially infeasible to run the ice arenas. The ice was never used in the Dome and was used for only a few years in Minett Hall. The neighbors felt cheated, believing they had contributed more money than they actually had, and they never forgave the Fair Association for what they considered a betrayal.

After months of hassles and investigation into the financial capabilities of the soccer complex developer, the project was abandoned, and subsequent inquiries into possible interest in the parcel, especially from hotel chains, were unfruitful.

Then in the early 2000s, the Fair Association received another offer, this time from Wegmans Food and Pharmacy, for a twenty-three acre tract of land at the front of the fairgrounds.

Wegmans is a major supermarket chain that started in Rochester and, in recent years, has expanded into the eastern part of the United States. At the time, it had seventeen stores in Monroe County, and one of its smallest and oldest stores was located across the street from the fairgrounds. Wegmans wanted to build a new, larger store that would have more of the services that people had come to expect, like a Market Café, a sub shop, an expanded take-out section, and a coffee counter. Wegmans began the process of getting permits to build, starting with the required town board meeting. People came out in droves, protesting this new store.

"We want to keep our small store," they insisted. And so the fight began.

Wegmans wasn't a novice at building new stores. They had an experienced marketing team that had conducted hundreds of town meetings, getting neighborhoods on board for their developments. Wegmans arranged a town meeting that would be held in the Dome, and one of their best marketers came out, prepared to answer questions. Halfway through the meeting, I could see the poor guy sweating. The attendees were vicious, and no matter what he said, he was shouted down. He later told me he had never encountered anything like it.

After three years of negotiations, with the town putting up all kinds of roadblocks, the offer was withdrawn. A lot of hard feeling ensued on the part of Wegmans toward Monroe County, and at one point, the president of Wegmans even threatened to move its headquarters out of Rochester. It was a blow as well to the Fair Association when the deal fell apart. We very much needed an influx of cash to upgrade buildings that were now thirty years old.

Several months later, my board had an idea for one last-ditch effort to broker the deal. Lucien Morin was a man with much influence and prestige in the area. He had been the Monroe County manager from 1984-1987, and he had once been an esteemed member of our board of directors. He was also personally acquainted with Bob Wegman, president of the grocery store chain. One of my board members asked Lou if he could use his influence to regenerate the deal.

Lou worked with Wegmans and with the town board and completed the negotiations in 2005 when the land sale contracts were finally signed. To sweeten the deal, the town obtained sidewalks, decorative light poles, and trees along a strip of land it hoped to develop into a town center. The neighbors got a new, modern Wegmans, which, as predicted, they came to love. Moreover, the Fair Association got a much-needed influx of cash that we used to renovate the fairgrounds.

With the renovations, we renamed the complex "The Fair and Expo Center," although that became a hopeless cause as most people still insisted on calling it "The Dome Center" or just "The Dome."

Throughout my years at the Fair Association, I worked to regain the trust of the community. We gave Good Neighbor Passes (which I sometimes thought was an oxymoron) to those people who lived within a half-mile of the fairgrounds. This allowed them to get into the fair for free and to get a discount to shows held at the Center. We allowed people to park without a fee during the town's Fourth of July fireworks. Without charge, we hosted the Guiding Eyes for the Blind Puppy Raiser program as well as 4-H dog obedience classes. We also hosted the town's "New Year's Eve Family Celebration," giving the town a drastically discounted rental rate, opened our lobby for voting on Election Day, and worked with the school district and the Chamber of Commerce. (I was eventually elected president of that organization and was selected Business Person of the Year in 2009, one of the achievements of which I am most proud.) I don't know if I was successful in my endeavor of getting people to like us again or if the people who were angry with the Fair Association finally moved away or just died, but in my later years the animosity seemed to have diminished.

Despite my ambivalent relationships with the politicos and the citizens of Henrietta, the business community seemed to embrace me, especially the hotel managers and sales people who wanted me to recommend their properties to show promoters. They always wanted to "do lunch" so they could showcase their hotels to me. I hated "doing lunch." First of all, I never knew who was supposed to pick up the tab. Secondly, I was always so nervous that my hands started shaking.

I've always believed that if you act as if you are calm and in control, people will believe that you are and will believe in your leadership. Eventually, you will come to believe it too, and this demeanor will become part of your persona. But one's insecurities still lurk in the recesses of the brain and sometimes show up in strange and unforeseen ways. Mine appeared when I had to eat in public. Since I tried to hide this flaw, my food choices were severely limited. Soup was out of the question, as was coffee that was served in cups where only one hand was required to hold it. If a mug was on the table, I breathed a sigh of relief because I could use two hands without looking like an idiot. I also didn't want salad because I envisioned green stuff stuck in my teeth, sandwiches were messy, and I didn't want anything dry that would stick in my throat. As a result, I usually ate little, cut things into minuscule bites, and was still eating the main course while everyone else was having dessert.

I remember one lunch in particular. One of the Henrietta hotels was under new management and had been remodeled. The manager asked me to come for lunch and to see the renovations. I obsessed about this Armageddon for weeks. When the day finally came, I somehow managed to get through lunch without spilling anything, and I made appropriate remarks on the tour, but I was vastly relieved when the manager finally walked me to the front door. Then I turned to him and said, "Good night" (it was one o'clock in the afternoon) and promptly walked into a plate glass window. It was not my best moment.

On another occasion, the Ryder Cup was scheduled to be played at Oak Hill Country Club, the most prestigious country club in Monroe County. The organizers wanted attendees to park their cars at the fairgrounds for the tournament. The people would then be shuttled to the golf course. The president of the event invited me to Oak Hill for lunch so that we could make the final arrangements. Most people would have been thrilled to be invited to Oak Hill for lunch. I dreaded it.

The weather on the day of the lunch was terrible. It was damp, and freezing rain had fallen earlier in the morning. I was determined, however, that I was not going to wear winter boots to Oak Hill. I parked in the country club's parking lot and began the trek to the front door, which was about a hundred yards away. The walkway was covered with a thin blanket of ice. I was wearing high heels. It took me ten minutes to walk that hundred yards as I crept along, holding onto low hanging tree branches and whatever else I could find. About five minutes into the walk, it began to drizzle, so by the time I made it to the front door, I was cold, wet, and my hair was plastered to my head in clumps as a result of coagulating hairspray. I don't remember anything about the lunch. All I could focus on was the fact that I had to renegotiate that walkway to get back to my car.

CHAPTER TWENTY-EIGHT

I've Got My Own Hard Hat!

With the sale of the land to Wegmans, we now had money to do some major renovations to the fairgrounds. It was not nearly enough, but it was a start.

Since it was a well-publicized fact that the Fair Association would have a sizable sum of money from the land sale, banks started courting me so that I would consider depositing the money in their particular establishments. This was called relationship marketing. I was taken out to lunch on a regular basis. Candy, cookies, and flowers were sent to the fairgrounds by the competing banks. I loved it. I was being treated like a millionaire! Eventually, the finance committee decided to split the money among three banks, and the courting ended.

We selected an architectural firm and a construction company, and then the renovations began in earnest. Back in the 1960s when I was in college, I had a little pillbox hat a la Jackie Kennedy. Now I had my own hard hat so I could walk in the construction zone.

The first thing we did was replace the problematic HVAC system with one that not only worked but that was also controlled by computer. At last, the offices and the upstairs meeting rooms had heat and air conditioning. What a treat! We were now officially in the 21st century.

Next, we replaced the marquee sign with one that was also controlled by a computer located in the front office. Heretofore, the maintenance staff had to manually change the lettering on the sign whenever we had a show. To accomplish this, the men needed to go up about twenty feet in the box of a forklift, no mean feat in a blizzard and no picnic during the heat of summer either.

Since the three buildings in the front of the fairgrounds were no longer on our property, we needed to build a new maintenance/

storage building. The architect attached the building perpendicularly to Minett Hall, but with that design, there was no way for trucks to pull into the building to unload for shows as there was not a sufficient turn radius at any of the overhead doors. I came up with the idea of splitting the new building in half with a covered drive-through between them. One half would be the shop area, and the other half would be for storage. At first, the idea was rejected as a whim of a woman who knew nothing about architecture, but the contractor revisited the idea and liked it, and it worked well for us. My maintenance supervisor, Myke, made me promise that I wouldn't use the drive-through or the maintenance building for the fair, as I had a habit of asking maintenance to empty out buildings if I needed extra space for exhibits. I promised, but after a couple of years, I needed a building to house the goats, and the drive-through was perfect for the rabbits. Myke just sighed and said that he figured it was just a matter of time. He already had a contingency plan. I loved that man.

We also demolished the narrow, dim connector hall between the Dome and Minett Hall and built a new, bright, and airy Welcome Court that now served as the main entrance to the facility. It was big enough to use for medium sized meetings and an excellent place for the flower show at the fair.

We paved some of the parking lots, installed underground water and electrical connections for the carnival, built a trailer park for the fair, and painted the roof, along with the inside and outside of all buildings. We also built new bathrooms with showers. The facility was starting to look pretty spiffy.

We needed a new horse arena and a new track as well. The horse arena looked great with new fencing, and the horse superintendents, Jay and Kirstie, worked with maintenance and a dedicated volunteer to get the footing right. The track, however, was more problematic.

Track events are essential to a fair, at least in Monroe County. The new Wegmans was to be located where the previous track had been. We really only needed a straightaway for demolition derbies, but one of our board members thought we should build an oval track for sprint cars. He said he knew of a construction company that could build it for a sum that was well within my budget. The cost of gasoline for their equipment and mileage to and from their company's garage would be an additional charge. This sounded doable. However, that summer, the price of gasoline began its surge to $6 a gallon, so the costs kept mounting as the company worked. Their monster construction equipment consumed gasoline as if it were water rather than liquid gold, and I was filling our 250 gallon gas tank twice a week to accommodate those thirsty monsters. When all was said and done, the project cost eight times what I had budgeted, and that made for quite a financially stressful time for me.

As with most construction projects, other overruns also ensued. The board decided that I should not have the power of approval for work change orders, which was regrettable. I was charged with managing the construction budget, but I was constantly being hit with bills for work changes of which I was unaware. Also, certain unknowns cost money: a new drainage line that the town required, fire doors in the Welcome Court that the state fire inspector demanded, and cement flooring in the maintenance building that a board member insisted upon and that I did not want. As a result, the project cost more than budgeted, and the deficit made my life hell for many years.

That aside, when the renovation project was finished, the fairgrounds looked great, and the fair took on a new look. New York State had a brand new commissioner of agriculture and markets, and he came to tour the fair the summer after the renovations were completed. He said he had never been to our fair before, and that he was really impressed by it. I felt so proud. When I first became executive director, the New York State Association of Agricultural Fairs' president had called us "an embarrassment to the industry." We had worked hard to change that image, and we were finally being recognized for all the innovations we had made.

CHAPTER TWENTY-NINE
Blue Skies and Sunny Days

After nearly twenty years, I finally decided to retire from the fair industry. I was sixty-seven years old, and the financial and political stressors were causing my blood pressure to run amok. Still, I felt pretty ambivalent about my decision. Sometimes, I counted down the remaining days with anticipation, and some days, the thought of retiring filled me with dread. After two decades of working sixty-hour weeks, what would I do with myself? Could I stay relevant? Would my brain turn to mush? Would I obsess over dust bunnies and become a cleaning freak?

My years at the fair were challenging and exhilarating and never dull. I met people from all walks of life, oversaw the renovation of the fairgrounds, and carried on through blizzards, tropical storms, ice storms, and droughts. I saw shows at the Fair and Expo Center grow and thrive, and I saw shows fade and fail. I worked with boards that were supportive and with boards that were difficult. I came to know people in the political world, the entertainment world, the advertising world, the construction world, the fair and carnival world, and the world of just plain folks who loved the fair and were willing to volunteer to make it better. I watched kids from our youth group grow into exemplary citizens and then bring their families to the fair as a new generation of enthusiasts.

Let's be honest. To be in the fair business, you have to be somewhat crazy. If you weren't crazy before you entered the business, you are certain to be nearly certifiable after twenty years in it. Each year, my staff, board, and I would come up with an idea of what we wanted the fair to be. Then we'd watch that idea grow until the fair took on a life of its own, at which point, we lost control and spent the rest of our time trying to keep our creation in check, sort of like Dr. Frankenstein. But that isn't what makes fair people crazy. The crazy part is that no matter how weird things get, fair people do the whole thing again the following year. Torrential downpours? We spit at rain! Electrical storms that knock your teeth out? Ha! Ninety-five degree temperatures? Don't be a sissy! That is either craziness or masochism, or maybe both.

Working for the Fair Association not only made me crazy but also both proud and humble. The people with whom I worked had an extraordinary emotional investment in the facility and in the fair, and everything we accomplished was the result of a super-human team effort. As a small nonprofit, there was never enough money to do what we wanted to do much less what was necessary. Yet the staff always soldiered on, finding ways to do the impossible with no resources and taking pride in finding solutions to the unsolvable. I was so lucky to have a staff like that.

I saw our fair change from what was dubbed "a sleazy carnival" and "an embarrassment to the industry" into one that was considered innovative, winning state and national recognition. My biggest disappointment was that our fair's attendance did not reflect the change in our stature.

Being a fair manager was not what I had planned to do in life, but I think it was what I was always meant to do. Corky once told me that I was "the heart of the fair," but I think it was just the opposite. I think the fair became my heart from the minute I stepped onto the fairgrounds in Santa Maria, California. The events and the people that were part of my life for twenty years enriched me, taught me, nurtured me, and filled my life with purpose.

As I sadly leave it all behind, I trust that the fair's future is in good hands. As a new generation takes on the mantle of leadership, I hope that the fair will grow and prosper, that it will be enjoyed by enthusiastic audiences, that it will have the support of the community, and, in the words of my carnival friends, that it will always be blessed with "blue skies and sunny days."

Afterword

The year after I retired, the fair board made the decision to sell the fairgrounds, which made me very sad. I always felt that we were simply custodians of the property and that we needed to protect it through thick and thin. To me, it was as if we were abandoning a sacred trust by selling it.

With the sale, the fair moved to Northampton Park in Ogden, a town on the opposite side of the county from its previous home in Henrietta. This was an unfortunate choice for a number of reasons. To begin with, the largest segment of the fair's patrons came from the local Henrietta community. Traveling to Ogden was not something a majority of traditional fairgoers were likely to undertake. Moreover, the second largest demographic were people from the city of Rochester. Since there was no public transportation to Ogden from downtown Rochester, this effectively eliminated another group of fairgoers. In order for the fair to succeed in its new location, it had to attract a whole new audience—no mean feat.

Another obstacle was that the neighbors around Northampton Park were adamantly and vocally against having the fair in the park. This created a lot of very negative publicity for the fair, which was detrimental to the board's goal of attracting a new and loyal audience.

The fair board also decided to have an "agriculture only" fair, eschewing the carnival and ignoring the hook that gets people to the event. This also eliminated a huge income source. As a result, the fair was very sparsely attended, even after the board eventually added some kiddie rides.

After four years in Ogden, the fair moved again, this time back to the east side of the county to the Rush Town Park. The board hopes that this will become the fair's permanent home, and they are presently in re-building mode—a daunting job. A fair can fail in one year, but it takes many years to build it back. I speak from experience.

In 2020 the COVID-19 pandemic presented another setback for the struggling fair. Like all fairs in New York State (and most in the country), the Monroe County Fair was forced to cancel the 2020 fair, only the fourth time in its history that it had happened. (There was no fair for three years during World War II.)

I don't know what will become of the Monroe County Fair. It has a proud tradition and has been in existence since 1823. In fact, it is one of the oldest fairs in the state and is even older than "the village of Rochester." It will take a dedicated fair board, hard work, long hours, and many volunteers to make the fair viable again. I sincerely hope that the board has the bone-deep commitment as well as the people-power to ensure that this traditional piece of the American landscape succeeds and soars, and once again, provides an annual snapshot of our community.

---The End---

Endnotes

1. Bob Marcott, "Track at Fairgrounds is Part of NASCAR History," *Rochester Democrat and Chronicle*, January 29, 2007, 17-18

2. "The Grange Movement," *The Gilder Lehrman Institute of American History AP US History Study Guide*, 2009-2019, http:// ap.gilderlehrman.org

3. International Association of Fairs and Expositions: "History of Fairs," https://www.fairsandexpos.com

4. Matt Braun, "Buffalo Bill Goosed the World's Fair," *True West History of the American Frontier*, April 2014

5. Outdoor Amusement Business Association: "Carnival Safety Statistics," 18100, https://www.oaba.org

6. Kaushik Patowary, "The Diving Horses of Atlantic City," Amusing Planet, November 13, 2017, https://www.amusingplanet.com

Acknowledgments

A book emanates from the author's mind, but what happens after the words are on paper has a lot to do with whether it stays tucked away in a file or becomes available for distribution. There are many people to thank for getting *Fair Lady* to that point.

First and foremost, many thanks to my editor and publisher, Nina Alvarez. When she said that she believed in my book and would like to publish it, I'm sure my screams could be heard for miles. I'm so grateful for her enthusiasm, for helping me to polish my writing, and for being excited right along with me. She made a difficult process easy and was patient with my attempts to navigate technology, admittedly not my strong suit.

Thanks also to my daughter, Wendy Ferrer, who was unfailingly accommodating during my numerous calls for help when my computer wouldn't cooperate or understand what I thought it should and for her advice and encouragement through the whole writing process.

My grandson Daniel Fratianni built my website, something completely out of my area of expertise, and he continues to assist me with social media. Taking on that aspect of the project was a huge relief and something I had no clue how to do on my own. Thanks, Daniel, for helping me through uncharted waters.

I asked my family to read *Fair Lady* and to give me feedback: what worked, what didn't, and what I was remembering incorrectly. Memories can sometimes fool you. Thanks to my son and daughter-in-law, Mike and Laura Tepper, who shared their memories of the fair with me, who corrected me when I was mistaken, and who gently nixed some of the more candid things I included.

I have written many articles, newsletters, and letters over the years. Thanks to all of my readers: friends, family and even strangers who took the time to tell me how much they enjoyed reading my missives. Your encouragement gave me the courage to write a book.

And lastly, thanks to my husband, Bruce, who endured many late meals because I was on a roll and didn't want to stop writing. He was completely supportive throughout the whole process, urging me to "go for it," knowing that both writing and the fair have been my passions for a long time. Putting the two together made sense to him.

About the Author

Orphaned at age sixteen, Frances Tepper put herself through the University of Southern California, graduating Phi Beta Kappa, *magna cum laude*. She married her high school sweetheart and returned to her home state, New York, raising children and working for 4-H as a program assistant. In 1992 Fran embarked on a career that would become her passion for the next twenty years: executive director of the Monroe County Fair and manager of the Fair Association's events center. During that time she published many columns and essays in local newspapers—and in the fair industry publication *Fairs and Expos*—about the life of the fair, writing with her trademark candor, insight, and humor. She was eventually elected president of the New York State Association of Agricultural Fairs as well as president of the

Henrietta Chamber of Commerce, which even named her Business Person of the Year in 2000. Fran retired after twenty years, but "fair fever" is still in her blood, and she can detect the aroma of fried dough from blocks away. She currently lives in Pittsford, New York with her husband. She has three grown children and six grandchildren and loves reading (often a book a day), traveling, video poker, and everything *Outlander*.

Made in the USA
Middletown, DE
19 March 2022

62841795R00128